C000178541

Religion, Peace and Conflict

through Christianity

Gordon Reid and Sarah K Tyler

OXFORD
UNIVERSITY PRESS

OXFORD
UNIVERSITY PRESS

Great Clarendon Street, Oxford, OX2 6DP, United Kingdom

Oxford University Press is a department of the University of Oxford.
It furthers the University's objective of excellence in research,
scholarship, and education by publishing worldwide. Oxford is a
registered trade mark of Oxford University Press in the UK and in
certain other countries

© Oxford University Press 2016

The moral rights of the authors have been asserted

First published in 2016

All rights reserved. No part of this publication may be reproduced,
stored in a retrieval system, or transmitted, in any form or by any
means, without the prior permission in writing of Oxford University
Press, or as expressly permitted by law, by licence or under terms
agreed with the appropriate reprographics rights organization.
Enquiries concerning reproduction outside the scope of the above
should be sent to the Rights Department, Oxford University Press,
at the address above.

You must not circulate this work in any other form and you must
impose this same condition on any acquirer

British Library Cataloguing in Publication Data
Data available

978-0-19-837044-4

10 9 8 7 6 5 4 3 2 1

Paper used in the production of this book is a natural, recyclable
product made from wood grown in sustainable forests. The
manufacturing process conforms to the environmental regulations
of the country of origin.

Printed in Great Britain by Bell and Bain Ltd., Glasgow

Links to third party websites are provided by Oxford in good faith
and for information only. Oxford disclaims any responsibility for the
materials contained in any third party website referenced in this work.

endorsed for
edexcel

In order to ensure that this resource offers high-quality support for
the associated Pearson qualification, it has been through a review
process by the awarding body. This process confirms that this resource
fully covers the teaching and learning content of the specification
or part of a specification at which it is aimed. It also confirms that it
demonstrates an appropriate balance between the development of
subject skills, knowledge and understanding, in addition to preparation
for assessment.

Endorsement does not cover any guidance on assessment activities or
processes (e.g. practice questions or advice on how to answer assessment
questions), included in the resource nor does it prescribe any particular
approach to the teaching or delivery of a related course.

While the publishers have made every attempt to ensure that advice on
the qualification and its assessment is accurate, the official specification
and associated assessment guidance materials are the only authoritative
source of information and should always be referred to for definitive
guidance.

Pearson examiners have not contributed to any sections in this resource
relevant to examination papers for which they have responsibility.

Examiners will not use endorsed resources as a source of material for
any assessment set by Pearson.

Endorsement of a resource does not mean that the resource is required
to achieve this Pearson qualification, nor does it mean that it is the only
suitable material available to support the qualification, and any resource
lists produced by the awarding body shall include this and other
appropriate resources.

Thank you

From the authors:

Our special thanks to Lois and Sarah at OUP – simply brilliant!

From the publisher:

OUP wishes to thank Philip H Robinson, RE Adviser to the CES,
Revd Dr Mark Griffiths, and Elisabeth Hoey for their valuable help
in reviewing and contributing to this book.

Contents

Edexcel GCSE Religious Studies

This book covers all you'll need to study for Edexcel GCSE Religious Studies Paper 2B: Religion, Peace and Conflict through Christianity. Whether you're studying for the full course or the short course, this book will provide the knowledge you'll need, as well as plenty of opportunities to prepare for your GCSE examinations.

GCSE Religious Studies provides the opportunity to study a truly fascinating subject: it will help you to debate big moral issues, understand and analyse a diverse range of opinions, as well as to think for yourself about the meaning of life.

How is the specification covered?

- The Edexcel specification is split into **four sections**:
  - *Christian Beliefs*
  - *Crime and Punishment*
  - *Living the Christian Life*
  - *Peace and Conflict*

This book has **four chapters** which match these sections. If you are taking the short course, you will only need to cover the first two sections: *Christian Beliefs*, and *Crime and Punishment*.

- Each of the four sections of the specification is split into **eight sub-sections**. These cover specific topics, like 'creation', or 'worship'. To support this, each chapter in this book is also split into the same eight sub-sections.

How to use this book

- So that you are fully prepared for your exams, you need to work through every chapter of this book (or just the first two for the short course). At the end of every topic there are exam-style questions which you should use to test your knowledge and practise your writing. Answering exam questions regularly, throughout your GCSE course, will really help you to be confident when exam time arrives.

- In the main topics there are lots of features to guide you through the material:

Specification focus provides you with the relevant description from the Edexcel specification, so that you can see exactly what the exam board expects you to know.

Support features help you to secure important knowledge, and **Stretch** features provide the opportunity for a challenge.

Build your skills are activities that focus on developing the skills you'll need for your exams, and consolidating the knowledge you'll need too.

A **compare and contrast** feature appears in 1.6 and 3.1. On these topics in your exam you may be required to compare Christian beliefs to another religion you are studying.

Exam-style questions gives two exam questions so that you can have a go at writing about the information you've studied in that topic. The letter at the start of each question tells you the question type (**a**, **b**, **c**, or **d**), and the number in brackets at the end tells you how many marks you are aiming for.

Sources of wisdom and authority will appear in boxes like this. Important, learnable phrases within a quote will often be in **bold**.

Useful terms are **orange** in the text and defined here. All of these terms are also provided in an alphabetical **glossary** at the end of the book.

Summary provides a short, bullet-pointed list of key information for ease of reference.

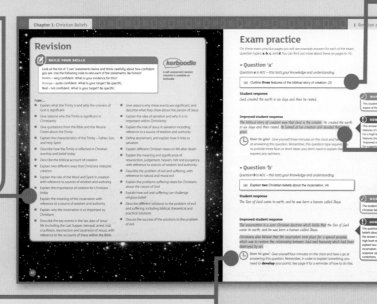

- At the end of every chapter there are a few pages called 'Revision and Exam practice'. These are designed to help you revise the information you have studied in that chapter, and coach you as you practise writing exam answers.

Four **exam-style questions** are provided – one for each of the question types **a**, **b**, **c**, and **d**.

Working through this revision checklist, and following up on anything you might have missed, will help you to make sure you've revised all of the important information from the chapter.

For each exam question, a sample **student answer** is provided, followed by an **improved** version so that you can be guided through improving your own answers.

What went well lists the good things about the first student response. **How to improve** lists its weaknesses, and suggests changes that should be made. These changes are reflected in the 'improved student response'.

Over to you! suggests that you have a go at answering the question yourself under exam conditions, and provides a few final exam tips.

Exam skills: What will the exams be like?

If you are studying the full course, you will sit **two** examinations, each **1 hour and 45 minutes** long. One exam will cover the content in this book (on Christianity), and the other will cover a second faith option.

If you are studying the short course, you will sit **two** examinations, each **50 minutes** long. One exam will cover the first two chapters of content in this book (on Christianity), and the other will cover a second faith option.

You must answer all of the questions on the exam paper.

Exam structure

Because this book covers just **one** of your two exams, the following information relates to that exam. For the full course exam, there will be **four questions** to answer. For the short course exam, there will be **two questions** to answer. Each question will relate to one of the four chapters in this book:

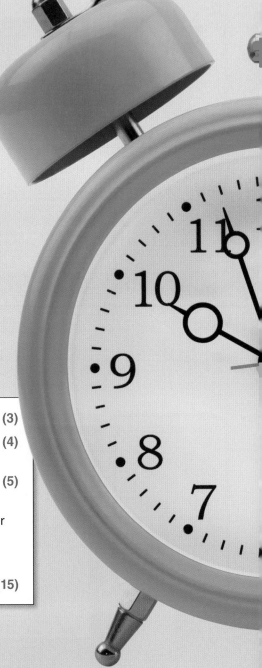

1. **Christian Beliefs**

2. **Crime and Punishment**

   Short course: answer two questions on these first two topics

3. **Living the Christian Life**

4. **Peace and Conflict**

   Full course: answer four questions, one for each of these four topics

Each question will be split into four parts: **a**, **b**, **c**, and **d**. For example, your first question on the exam (covering *1. Christian Beliefs*) could be something like this:

> **1** (a) Outline **three** features of the Trinity. (3)
>
> (b) Explain **two** types of evil. (4)
>
> (c) Explain **two** reasons why the resurrection is important to Christians. In your answer you must refer to a source of wisdom and authority. (5)
>
> (d) 'Christianity provides no solutions to the problem of evil and suffering.' Evaluate this statement considering arguments for and against. In your response you should:
> - refer to Christian teachings
> - refer to different Christian points of view
> - reach a justified conclusion. (15)

The 'a' question

The 'a' question will always start with the words 'Outline **three**…' or 'State **three**', and the maximum number of marks awarded will be three marks. For example:

> **1** **(a)** Outline **three** features of the Trinity. **(3)**

The 'b' question

The 'b' question will always start with the words 'Explain **two**…' or 'Describe **two**…', and the maximum number of marks awarded will be four marks. For example:

> **(b)** Explain **two** types of evil. **(4)**

The 'c' question

The 'c' question will always start with the words 'Explain **two**…', and will ask you to refer to a source of wisdom and authority. The maximum number of marks awarded will be five marks. For example:

> **(c)** Explain **two** reasons why the resurrection is important to Christians. In your answer you must refer to a source of wisdom and authority. **(5)**

The 'd' question

The 'd' question will always start with a statement of opinion that you are asked to evaluate. These questions will sometimes be out of 12 marks, and sometimes be out of 15 marks (see page 11, 'Written communication', to find out why!). For example:

> **(d)** 'Christianity provides no solutions to the problem of evil and suffering.' Evaluate this statement considering arguments for and against. In your response you should:
> - refer to Christian teachings
> - refer to different Christian points of view
> - reach a justified conclusion. **(15)**

Know your question types!

…that way, nothing in your exam will take you by surprise!

Exam skills: How will the exams be marked?

When you're revising and practising using exam questions, it will really help you to understand how you'll be marked. If you know what the examiners are looking for, then you're more likely to do well!

Assessment Objectives

Examiners will mark your work using two Assessment Objectives: Assessment Objective 1 (AO1), and Assessment Objective 2 (AO2). The two Assessment Objectives are described in the table below.

	Students must:	Weighting
AO1	Demonstrate knowledge and understanding of religion and belief, including: • beliefs, practices and sources of authority • influence on individuals, communities and societies • similarities and differences within and/or between religions and beliefs.	50%
AO2	Analyse and evaluate aspects of religion and belief, including their significance and influence.	50%

You need to remember that 50% of the marks available in your exam will be awarded for demonstrating **knowledge and understanding of religion and belief** (AO1), and 50% of the marks available will be awarded for **analysing and evaluating aspects of religion and belief** (AO2).

Marking the 'a' question

'Outline/State' questions are assessed using Assessment Objective 1 (knowledge) only. These questions require you to provide three facts or short ideas: **you don't need to explain them or express any opinions**. For example, in answer to the question 'Outline **three** features of the Trinity', your three responses could be:

1. There is one God in three persons (1)

2. Each person is fully God (1)

3. Each person is different from the other persons (1)

For each response, you would receive 1 mark. You're not expected to spend time explaining what the Trinity is: the question only asks you to give three features.

Marking the 'b' question

Like the 'a' question, 'b' questions are assessed using Assessment Objective 1 (knowledge) only. However, 'b' questions start with 'Explain' or 'Describe', which means you will need to show **development** of ideas. For example, if the question is 'Explain **two** types of evil' you might think you just need to state the two types, but this means you can only be awarded **a maximum of two marks**:

Type 1: One type of evil is called natural evil (1)

Type 2: Another type of evil is called moral evil (1)

The types given above are correct, but the student would only score 2 marks out of 4. In order to fully **explain** these reasons, you need to show some **development**. For example:

Type 1: One type of evil is called natural evil (1), **which means evil caused by nature, e.g. earthquakes (1)**

Type 2: Another type of evil is called moral evil (1), **which means evil caused by humans, e.g. murder (1)**

Each of the above points are now developed, and would receive 2 marks each, totalling **4 marks**.

CONNECTIVES

A **connective** helps you to develop your basic answer. There are lots of different types of connective (therefore/ because/and/consequently/a result of this is/this means that). However, take care not to simply repeat the question and then use a connective, as that is not a developed answer and is only worth one mark. For example, 'Christians believe in two types of evil, **and** one of these is called natural evil' would only receive one mark despite the use of a connective.

Marking the 'c' question

Like the 'a' and 'b' questions, 'c' questions are assessed using Assessment Objective 1 (knowledge) only. 'C' questions are very similar to 'b' questions (they begin with 'Explain **two**' and require two developed points), but they have one crucial difference. For an extra mark, you are expected to include a reference to a **source of wisdom and authority**, which could be a quotation from/reference to the Bible or another important source within Christianity. For example, here's a student answer to a five-mark question:

> (c) Explain **two** reasons why the resurrection is important to Christians. In your answer you must refer to a source of wisdom and authority. **(5)**
>
> Christians believe that Jesus' resurrection allows their sins to be forgiven **(1)**. Therefore, they can have a true relationship with God again **(1)**. If Christians repent, they will be forgiven (Luke 24: 47) **(1)**.
>
> Jesus' resurrection means that death is not the end **(1)**; this means that he showed that death could be overcome and he paved the way for Christians to be with God **(1)**.

You need to write **two** developed points, one of which needs to be supported by a source of wisdom and authority. Setting out your writing in two paragraphs makes it clear that it is two developed points. You could directly quote a source, or you could just include the reference (as in the above student answer).

Marking the 'd' question

The 'd' question is marked using AO2 (analysis/evaluation). These questions specifically ask you to evaluate a statement. Evaluating a statement means that you are weighing up how good or true it is. The best way to evaluate something is to consider different opinions on the matter – and this is exactly what the question asks you to do. When you are planning your answer, you need to remember to do the following:

- Refer to Christian teachings – for instance core beliefs and important sources of wisdom and authority
- Ensure that different viewpoints are included either from within Christianity or non-religious views, and ensure that relevant ethical or philosophical arguments are referred to (the question will make it clear which of these will be required in your answer)
- Ensure that you include a justified conclusion – in other words, your final decision on the matter having considered different viewpoints.

If you don't refer to different viewpoints, **you cannot get more than half of the marks**.

The examiner will mark your answer using a **mark scheme**, similar to the one below.

Level 1 (1–3 marks)	• Basic information or reasons about the issue are identified and can be explained by some religious or moral understanding. • Opinions are given but not fully explained.
Level 2 (4–6 marks)	• Some information or reasons about the issue are loosely identified and can be explained by limited religious or moral understanding. • Opinions are given which attempt to support the issue but are not fully explained or justified.
Level 3 (7–9 marks)	• Information given clearly describes religious information/issues, leading to coherent and logical chains of reasoning **that consider different viewpoints**. These are supported by an accurate understanding of religion and belief. • The answer contains coherent and reasoned judgements of many, but not all, of the elements in the question. Judgements are supported by a good understanding of evidence, leading to a partially justified conclusion.
Level 4 (10–12 marks)	• The response critically deconstructs religious information/issues, leading to coherent and logical chains of reasoning **that consider different viewpoints**. These are supported by a sustained, accurate, and thorough understanding of religion and belief. • The answer contains coherent and reasoned judgements of the full range of elements in the question. Judgements are fully supported by the comprehensive use of evidence, leading to a fully justified conclusion.

ARE YOU READY?

Written communication

Some of the marks in your exam will be awarded purely for the quality of your 'written communication'. Written communication includes your use of correct **spelling, punctuation and grammar**, as well as the use of **specialist terminology**.

These marks will be awarded in questions **1(d)** and **3(d)**: these are the long essay questions on topics 1 and 3 (*Christian Beliefs* and *Living the Christian Life*). Whereas 'd' questions in topics 2 and 4 are out of 12 marks, these will be out of **15 marks**, and the extra 3 marks in each question are awarded solely for your written communication. You'll know which questions these are in the exam because they will be shown with an asterisk (*) and have a really clear instruction above them:

> **In this question, 3 of the marks awarded will be for your spelling, punctuation and grammar and your use of specialist terminology.**
>
> *(d) 'Christianity provides no solutions to the problem of evil and suffering.'
>
> Evaluate this statement considering arguments for and against. In your response you should:
> - refer to Christian teachings
> - refer to different Christian points of view
> - reach a justified conclusion. (15)

In these questions:

- 0 marks are awarded if there are considerable errors or irrelevant information
- 1 mark is awarded for reasonable accuracy and limited use of religious terms
- 2 marks are awarded for considerable accuracy and a good number of specialist terms
- 3 marks are awarded for consistent accuracy and a wide range of specialist terms.

Good written communication is always important, but you will only receive marks for it in questions **1(d)** and **3(d)**. Therefore, you should allow yourself time in your exam to check these two essays carefully and amend any errors.

Introduction to Christianity

What is Christianity?

Christianity is the main religious tradition in Great Britain. Other religious traditions include Islam, Buddhism, Judaism, Hinduism, and Sikhism.

Central to Christianity is a man named Jesus, whose existence in first-century Palestine has been recorded by early Roman and Jewish scholars. The life and impact of Jesus is described in the New Testament of the Bible – the Christian holy book – including the claim that Jesus is the Son of God, and accounts of the work of his followers, the early Christians.

What do Christians believe?

Christians believe in one God in three persons: God the Father, God the Son (who came to earth as Jesus), and God the Holy Spirit (see 1.1). Christians believe that God loves them, and wants to have a relationship with them. They believe that, because of this love, he sent Jesus to live amongst them, to die on a cross and be raised to life three days later. They believe he did this to free humanity from sin, and make it possible for them to spend eternity with God in heaven (see 1.3–1.5).

While he was on earth, Jesus chose twelve specific followers, who are known within Christianity as the apostles, or disciples. He also had many other followers, however, including women and children. According to the Bible, after his death and resurrection Jesus' followers gathered in Jerusalem, and the number of followers grew quickly from hundreds to thousands as the apostles began to teach about Jesus and the things they had experienced.

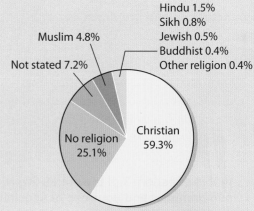

Hindu 1.5%
Sikh 0.8%
Jewish 0.5%
Buddhist 0.4%
Other religion 0.4%
Muslim 4.8%
Not stated 7.2%
No religion 25.1%
Christian 59.3%

The 2011 England and Wales census asked people, 'What is your religion?'. This pie chart shows how people responded.

What are the different groups within Christianity?

Today, Christianity has followers all over the world. The word 'denomination' is used to describe a particular group within Christianity. There are many different denominations which you will learn about in this book.

The Catholic Church and the Orthodox Church

The Catholic Church was the only Christian Church until 1054CE. Around 1054CE, a new denomination was formed, one that we now refer to as the Orthodox Church. There were many reasons why this split occurred, but a key reason was that the Orthodox Church did not believe the Pope (the leader of the Catholic Church) should have ultimate authority.

The Protestant denominations

In 1517, Martin Luther, a Catholic priest, challenged a range of Catholic practices. His followers were called 'Lutherans', and shortly after, the Lutheran Church was formed. It was, in effect, the first of the Protestant denominations, which developed as a 'protest' against the practices of the Catholic Church.

Since that time, a number of Protestant denominations have formed, for example:

- The Church of England (sometimes called the Anglican Church)
- The Baptist Church
- The Methodist Church
- The Salvation Army
- Pentecostal denominations.

New denominations continue to form today, and usually come out of existing denominations. They are formed because of differences over two main factors:

1. Governance (the way the denomination is structured)

2. Theology (what the denomination believes).

Today, it is very important to understand that there is a lot of overlap among denominations, particularly the larger denominations. For example, charismatic worship (traditionally associated with the Pentecostal church) can be found in Anglican and Catholic churches (see 3.1). Many churches also work together, which is called ecumenism (see 3.7).

Christians in Great Britain today

From a dozen people in Jerusalem in the first century, Christianity now has more than 2.4 billion believers all over the world. In Great Britain, Christianity is still the main religious tradition, despite a growing number of people who do not identify with any particular religion.

The study of Christianity will enable you to develop a greater understanding of the practice of Christianity in Great Britain and the wider world, and to consider the values held by Christians. This book provides you with opportunities to make your own observations, raise questions, and draw personal conclusions about various teachings, beliefs and important issues.

Chapter 1:
Christian Beliefs

What is the Trinity?

The **Trinity** is unique to Christianity. It is the belief that there is only one God, but that he exists in three 'persons':

● God the Father

● God the Son

● God the **Holy Spirit** (sometimes called the Holy Ghost).

Each of these three persons is fully God, but they are not *three* Gods – they are *one* God.

The Nicene Creed

The Nicene Creed is a statement of belief that many Christians recite in church. It says of the Trinity:

> ❝ We believe in one God, the Father, the Almighty, maker of heaven and earth […] We believe in one Lord, **Jesus Christ**, the only Son of God, eternally **begotten** of the Father […] We believe in the Holy Spirit, the giver of life, who proceeds from the Father and the Son. ❞

The Nicene Creed reveals the following about the nature of the Trinity:

● **God the Father** is the creator of the universe and is the 'Almighty' (having complete power).

● **God the Son** is Jesus Christ who is 'Lord' and the Son of the Father.

● **God the Holy Spirit** comes from the Father and the Son. Christians believe the Holy Spirit is the 'giver of life', meaning he is spiritually active in the world, he helps them to know God and worship him, and he equips and empowers believers.

What is the 'oneness' of God?

The Trinity can be a difficult idea to understand. For example, how can God be 'one' and 'three' at the same time? Think of the Trinity like diagram **A**. There is one God. There are three different persons, each of whom is different from the other two but each of whom is fully God. This is the special 'oneness' of God.

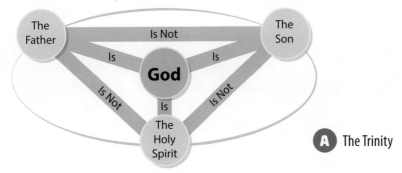

A The Trinity

SPECIFICATION FOCUS

The Trinity: the nature and significance of the Trinity as expressed in the Nicene Creed; the nature and significance of the oneness of God; the nature and significance of each of the Persons individually: including reference to Matthew 3: 13–17; how this is reflected in Christian worship and belief today.

This quotation contains some difficult ideas: **SUPPORT**

● **'eternally begotten'** means that the Son of God has always existed, and is in a relationship as Son of the Father.

● **'proceeds from the Father'** means the Holy Spirit comes directly (proceeds) from God. Like the Son of God, the Holy Spirit is not *made by* God but *is* God.

USEFUL TERMS

Begotten: born of

Holy Spirit: the Spirit of God, who gives the power to understand and worship

Jesus Christ: the Son of God, who came into the world as a human being

Trinity: God as one being, in three persons

The persons of the Trinity

The word 'Trinity' does not appear in the Bible. However, there is one event, described in the Gospel of Matthew, where the persons of the Trinity do all appear together. This is when Jesus is baptised before beginning his ministry in the world:

> ❛As soon as **Jesus** was baptised, he went up out of the water. At that moment heaven was opened, and he saw **the Spirit of God** descending like a dove and alighting on him. And a **voice from heaven** said, "This is my Son, whom I love; with him I am well pleased."❜
> *(Matthew 3: 16–17)*

This is important because it shows the Trinity working together as one – Jesus is baptised to begin his ministry, the Father speaks his approval, and the Holy Spirit, with the power of the Father, enables Jesus to begin his work.

B *The Baptism of Christ*, a painting by Paolo Veronese (c.1580ᴄᴇ–1588ᴄᴇ)

Look at this painting and the corresponding story in the Bible (*Matthew 3: 13–17*). Can you find three different symbolic ideas? Why do you think these ideas are important for Christians?

STRETCH

The Bible highlights the importance of each person of the Trinity and how they can be understood and worshipped by Christians today.

> ❛Therefore go and make disciples of all nations, baptising them in the name of the Father and of the Son and of the Holy Spirit.❜
> *(Matthew 28: 19)*

> ❛The grace of our Lord Jesus Christ, and the love of God, and the fellowship of the Holy Spirit be with you.❜
> *(2 Corinthians 13: 14)*

How is the Trinity reflected in worship and belief today?

Christians use the Trinity as the guide for worship and belief. Christians believe that the Trinity displays God's loving nature, which impacts on their worship.

- **God the Father:** Christians believe that God the Father, as the creator, cares for all that he has made. They pray to him in the knowledge that he cares about them and is powerful, like Jesus did in the Lord's Prayer: 'This, then, is how you should pray: "Our Father in heaven, hallowed be your name …"' (Matthew 6: 9).

- **God the Son:** Christians believe that, around 5BCE, God the Son became a human being (see 1.3), and he was given the name Jesus. Christians believe Jesus is their saviour, friend and role-model. They follow the example set by Jesus, who came into the world to teach people how to live lives of goodness, love and faith. A core belief about Jesus is that he died to take the punishment for the sins of **humanity** (see 1.4–1.5). Worship is therefore often happy and joyful, as Christians express their thanks to God for forgiving their sins and to Jesus for the sacrifice he made.

- **God the Holy Spirit:** Christians believe that the Holy Spirit is their comforter and guide. They believe that the Holy Spirit lives in their hearts and not only enables them to lead good lives and make the right moral choices, but also helps them to praise and worship God. **Charismatic** churches, such as the Pentecostal Church and an increasing number of Anglican churches, will ask the Holy Spirit to enable them to worship using **spiritual gifts**. These church services are often less formal and involve dancing and creative expression.

USEFUL TERMS

Charismatic: a power given by God, e.g. inspired teaching

Humanity: all human beings

Spiritual gifts: gifts given by God to believers, e.g. speaking in 'tongues', a special language

C A church meeting that involves charismatic worship. Can you identify any special features of this kind of worship?

Christians believe that the Trinity is a model of mutual love and perfect unity. It helps Christians to understand more about relationships because the Trinity is very similar to the way they live. They are not alone, they have families and friends who they can talk to, enjoy time with, and often love. In the same way, Christians believe the Trinity is a loving relationship with each of the three persons relating to the others – just like a family. This 'oneness' is reflected in Christian songs and hymns:

> ❛Shine, Jesus, shine, fill this land with the Father's glory. Blaze, Spirit, blaze, set our hearts on fire.❜
> *'Shine, Jesus, Shine', by Graham Kendrick*

> ❛Holy, holy, holy, Lord God Almighty [...] God in three persons, blessed Trinity!❜
> *'Holy, Holy, Holy', by Reginald Heber*

Christians are baptised 'in the name of the Father and of the Son and of the Holy Spirit' (*Matthew 28: 19*) (see 3.2) and sometimes the sign of the cross is made with a hand gesture in three movements, reflecting the Trinity.

BUILD YOUR SKILLS

1   In pairs, write down in your own words how you would describe the Trinity. As you do so, consider the following aspects:
   - How can God be 'one' and 'three' at the same time?
   - How are the three persons different from each other?
   - Do you think the idea of the Trinity makes God easier or harder to understand? Why?

2   a   What are the reasons why Christians feel that they should believe in the Trinity?
   b   How does the idea of the Trinity help Christians?

3   Look at image **D**. How would the Holy Spirit enable Christians to respond in this situation?

EXAM-STYLE QUESTIONS

b   Explain **two** Christian beliefs about the Trinity. (4)
c   Explain **two** reasons why the concept of the Trinity is important for Christians. In your answer you must refer to a source of wisdom and authority. (5)

SUMMARY

- Christians believe in the concept of the Trinity. God is one, God is in three persons (Father, Son and Holy Spirit), and each person is fully God.
- In the Bible, all three persons were present at the baptism of Jesus (*Matthew 3: 13–17*).
- Christians worship God the Father and Jesus Christ in a formal way or in private, and many believe that the Holy Spirit helps them to worship in the most fulfilling way.

D

What is the biblical account of creation?

There are two accounts of creation in Genesis, the first book of the Bible. The first, in *Genesis 1:1–2:3*, contains the story of the creation of the earth by God in six days. God speaks and things happen:

SPECIFICATION FOCUS

The creation of the universe and of humanity: the biblical account of creation and divergent ways in which it may be understood by Christians, including as literal and metaphorical; the role of the Word and Spirit in creation including John 1: 1–18 and Genesis 1–3; the importance of creation for Christians today.

Day 2 Water and sky

Day 1 Heavens, earth, light and dark

Day 3 Land and plant life

Day 6 Land animals and humans

Day 4 Sun, moon, and stars

Day 5 Fish and birds

A The *Genesis 1:1–2:3* account of creation: God created the earth in six days and rested on the seventh day

The second account, in *Genesis 2:4–3:23*, is different because it concentrates on the development of humans:

1

"Then **the Lord God formed a man** from the dust of the ground and breathed into his nostrils the breath of life, and the man became a living being." *(Genesis 2: 7)*

2

"The Lord God took the man and placed him in **the Garden of Eden** to work it and take care of it." *(Genesis 2: 15)*

3
"And the Lord God commanded the man, "You are free to eat from any tree in the garden; but **you must not eat from the tree of the knowledge of good and evil**, for when you eat from it you will certainly die."" *(Genesis 2: 16–17)*

6
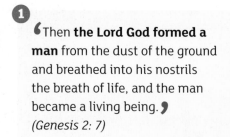
"So the Lord God banished him from the Garden of Eden..." *(Genesis 3: 23)*

5
"When the woman saw that the fruit of the tree was good [...] **she took some and ate it. She also gave some to her husband...**" *(Genesis 3: 6–7)*

4
"Then **the Lord God made a woman** from the rib he had taken out of the man..." *(Genesis 2: 22)*

How can the biblical account of creation be understood in different ways?

There are differing views on exactly what the Bible means in the accounts of creation:

- **The metaphorical view:** Many Christians believe this account is a metaphor, and is not literally true. They would argue that it is a story to help people to understand that God is the creator of all things.
- **The literal view:** Others believe that the Bible account is literally true and God created the world exactly as the Bible says. This is called **creationism**. Creationists believe that the Bible is the sacred word of God and believe that it should be interpreted literally where possible. Young Earth Creationists believe that the world was made in six days approximately 10,000 years ago.

> **USEFUL TERMS**
>
> **Creationism:** the belief that the world was created in a literal six days and that Genesis is a scientific/historical account of the beginning of the world

What is the role of the Word and Spirit?

The Bible teaches that God the Father, Son and Holy Spirit – the Trinity – were all involved in the act of creation.

The Word

In the New Testament, the Gospel of John says:

> ❝**In the beginning was the Word**, and the Word was with God, and the Word was God.❞
> *(John 1: 1)*

> ❝**Through him** [the Word] **all things were made** […] In him was life…❞
> *(John 1: 3–4)*

> Read the full quotation in *John 1: 1–18*. Can you explain how this passage links to the ideas of **incarnation** and **salvation**? (See 1.3 and 1.5.) **STRETCH**

But who is the 'Word'? The answer is Jesus, because the Gospel goes on to say, 'The Word became flesh and made his dwelling among us…' (*John 1: 14*). So Christians believe that God the Son (Jesus) was with God the Father at the start, acting in the creation. They believe he is the source of life.

The Book of Genesis also says that God created not by using his hands, but by speaking: 'God said…' (*Genesis 1: 3*). Of course, what he speaks are words – hence Jesus is 'the Word'. As it says in the Book of Psalms, 'By the word of the Lord were the heavens made…' (*Psalm 33: 6*).

The Spirit

In the Book of Genesis it says that during the act of creation the 'Spirit of God was hovering over the waters' (*Genesis 1: 2*). This image describes the Holy Spirit as present in creation to protect what has, and will be, created. The Spirit (Hebrew: 'breath') of God guards creation.

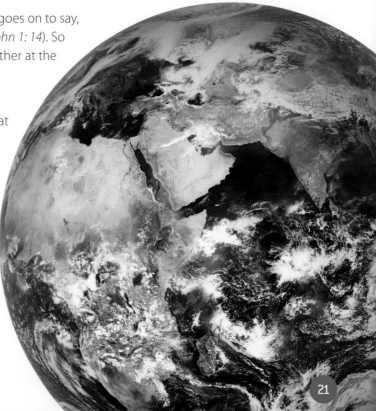

Why is creation important for Christians today?

The relationship between humans and their creator

The Bible says that man and woman were created in the image of God. Christians therefore believe that human beings are important to God, as he expressed something of himself in creating them.

- At the start, when God creates man and woman (Adam and Eve), they walk and talk with God in a relationship of love and devotion. God said, 'I give you every seed-bearing plant [...] and every tree' (*Genesis 1: 29*).

- God gave Adam and Eve **free will**, but they chose to disobey God by eating from the forbidden tree. The relationship of mutual love and trust between God and humanity was broken.

- God therefore sent Adam and Eve out of the Garden of Eden and ordered them to work the ground: 'By the sweat of your brow you will eat your food [...] for dust you are and to dust you will return' (*Genesis 3: 19*).

- Today, Christians believe that they have a personal and loving relationship with God and that they can pray to God for guidance. They believe that God has given humanity the opportunity to care for creation, with God's guidance and help.

The relationship between humans and the rest of creation

Christians believe that:

- God gave humans the responsibility to look after the world as his 'stewards' (*Genesis 1: 26*). This means that they are to have authority over the animals, plants and other resources.

- God blessed humans and said, 'Be fruitful and increase in number; fill the earth and subdue it. Rule over the fish in the sea and the birds in the sky and over every living creature that moves on the ground.' (*Genesis 1: 28*).

- They should care for the environment so that the world can be passed on to future generations as a better place than when they found it. This is called **stewardship**.

Christians believe humans should:
- treat animals and the land kindly
- leave the world better than they found it
- share things fairly
- be judged by God on their actions.

This means humans should take on certain duties:
- reduction of pollution
- **conservation** of resources
- sharing with the poor
- conservation of the **environment**.

USEFUL TERMS

Conservation: protecting something from being damaged or destroyed

Environment: the surroundings in which plants and animals live and on which they depend for life

Free will: having the freedom to choose what to do

Stewardship: looking after something so it can be passed on to the next generation

STRETCH

Interestingly, at the time of Jesus, the people of Israel would celebrate a 'Year of Jubilee', when no crops were planted, to give the land a well-earned rest: 'The fiftieth year shall be a jubilee for you; do not sow and do not reap' (*Leviticus 25: 11*). Is this a good idea? Why/why not?

BUILD YOUR SKILLS

1 Copy and complete the following table for the main ideas about creation given in this unit. Three ideas have been suggested for you. **SUPPORT**

Term/idea	What does it mean?	Why is it important for Christians?
Creation		
Stewardship		
Made in the image of God		

2 Which aspects of the biblical account of creation are **a** most convincing and **b** least convincing? Why?

3 Is God's punishment of Adam and Eve fair and just? Why/why not?

4 Look at this car used by campaigners, in image **C**.
   a What is the message being conveyed? Is it pro-creationist or anti-creationist?
   b Make a list of arguments that support creationism and a list of arguments against. Which are the most convincing arguments, and why?

5 What comes first, stopping pollution or fulfilling human needs? For example, is it right to shut down a polluting factory if it means 1000 people will lose their jobs? **STRETCH**

C

SUMMARY

- There are two accounts of how God created the world and humanity in the Book of Genesis, and there is another account in *John 1: 1–18*.

- Some Christians believe these accounts are literally true, whilst others think they are metaphorical.

- Christians believe that God has made them stewards, with a duty to care for the world and its resources.

EXAM-STYLE QUESTIONS

a Outline **three** Christian beliefs about creation. (3)

d 'A Christian should believe the world was made in seven days.' Evaluate this statement considering arguments for and against. In your response you should:
   - refer to Christian teachings
   - refer to different Christian points of view
   - reach a justified conclusion. (15)

1.3 The incarnation

What is the incarnation?

Christians believe that Jesus Christ is the Son of God, who came down to earth to live as a man from around 5BCE to around 33CE. This is called the **incarnation**. You will be learning about the life and significance of Jesus in 1.3–1.5.

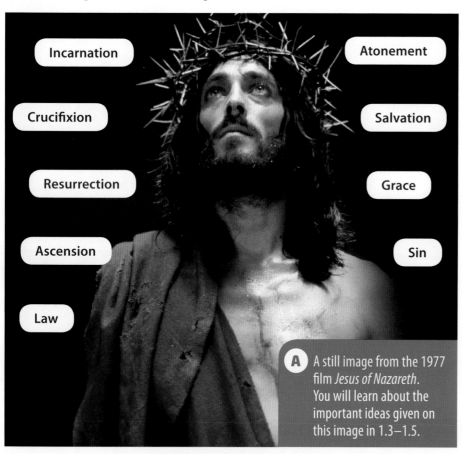

Incarnation

Crucifixion

Resurrection

Ascension

Law

Atonement

Salvation

Grace

Sin

A A still image from the 1977 film *Jesus of Nazareth*. You will learn about the important ideas given on this image in 1.3–1.5.

SPECIFICATION FOCUS

The incarnation: the nature and importance of the person of Jesus Christ as the incarnate Son of God; the biblical basis of this teaching, including John 1: 1–18 and 1 Timothy 3: 16 and its significance for Christians today.

USEFUL TERMS

Incarnation: to take on flesh; God becomes a human being

How is the incarnation shown in the Bible?

For Christians, God the Son, the second person of the Trinity, became a human being in Jesus of Nazareth. The Bible describes the incarnation in this way:

> ❛The virgin will conceive and give birth to a son, and **they will call him Immanuel**.❜
> *(Matthew 1: 23)*

> ❛The Word became flesh and made his dwelling among us.❜
> *(John 1: 14)*

The Bible teaches that God the Son came into the world to live among people, show them what God was like and enable them to have a relationship with him.

The word **incarnation** means 'to take on flesh': God takes on a physical human form in order to be more accessible to humanity. **SUPPORT**

Immanuel means 'God with us'.

The Bible also describes the incarnation as a great mystery, because there are aspects of it that are amazing and beyond human understanding:

> ❛Beyond all question, **the mystery from which true godliness springs is great**: He appeared in the flesh, was vindicated by the Spirit, was seen by angels, was preached among the nations, was believed on in the world, was taken up in glory.❜
> *(1 Timothy 3: 16)*

What is the importance of the incarnation for Christians today?

- Christians believe that Jesus is God incarnate. They believe Jesus came into the world to enable the relationship between God and humanity to be restored (see 1.2). The incarnation is therefore important for Christians because it allows them to have a relationship with God.

- Christians believe that the incarnation shows that God loves the world and the people in it. This is what they celebrate during Christmas (see 3.5). Christians celebrate the incarnation on Christmas Day by singing Christmas carols and remembering the story of the birth of Jesus.

- Christians believe that, as a human, Jesus could understand humanity and its problems, and identify with their suffering.

 B Christians take part in an all-age 'Christingle' service at Fawley All Saints Church in Hampshire, which celebrates Jesus as the 'light of the world'

What aspects of the incarnation are mysterious **STRETCH** and why? Refer to this quotation from *1 Timothy* in your answer.

Vindicated means proven to be true or genuine. **SUPPORT**

BUILD YOUR SKILLS

1 a With a partner or in a small group, write down a list of reasons why the incarnation might be true, and a list for why it might be false.
   b Which are the strongest reasons and why?

2 Why is the incarnation important for Christians? Explain two reasons in your own words. Refer to a source of wisdom and authority.

EXAM-STYLE QUESTIONS

a Outline **three** Christian beliefs about Jesus. (3)
c Explain **two** Christian beliefs about the incarnation of Jesus. In your answer you must refer to a source of wisdom and authority. (5)

SUMMARY

- Christians believe that God came into the world as Jesus, a man. This is called the incarnation.

- The purpose of the incarnation was to enable human beings to have a relationship with God.

1.4 The last days of Jesus' life

SPECIFICATION FOCUS

The last days of Jesus' life: the Last Supper, betrayal, arrest, trial, crucifixion, resurrection and ascension of Jesus; the accounts of these within the Bible, including Luke 22–24 and the significance of these events to understanding the person of Jesus Christ.

What happened in the last days of Jesus' life and why are these events important?

The Last Supper and betrayal

The evening before he died, Jesus and his disciples had a meal together, which Christians call the Last Supper. At the meal, Jesus spoke about his forthcoming death. He tried to prepare the disciples for the future by teaching them to serve one another (*Luke 22: 26–27*). He explained that after he was gone he would send the Holy Spirit to 'teach you all things and remind you of everything I have said to you' (*John 14: 26*).

Jesus also gave the disciples bread to eat and wine to drink. He said that they are his 'body' and his 'blood'. They represented his sacrifice –'This is my body given for you' (*Luke 22: 19*) (see 3.2).

Jesus also knew that one of the disciples would betray him, having him arrested by the Jewish authorities. He said to the disciples: 'the hand of him who is going to betray me is with mine on the table. [...] But woe to that man who betrays [me]' (*Luke 22: 21–22*). It was Judas Iscariot who betrayed him.

For Christians, these events highlight that Jesus' teachings had begun to come true – he knew what was going to happen. Christians remember the Last Supper when they take part in the Eucharist (see 3.2).

STRETCH

Read the full story in *Luke 22: 7–38*. What can Christians learn about the person of Jesus from this passage?

A *The Sacrament of the Last Supper* by Salvador Dalí (1955)

Jesus' betrayal, arrest, and trial

Jesus and the disciples planned to spend the night in a garden called Gethsemane. In the middle of the night, Judas Iscariot brought an armed crowd to take Jesus away. Judas identified Jesus to the authorities by kissing him (*Luke 22: 47–48*).

Jesus was taken before the Jewish High Council, called the Sanhedrin. They found Jesus guilty of blasphemy for claiming to be the Son of God. They believed that this was a great crime which should be punished by death.

After this, the Jewish leaders took Jesus to the Roman governor, Pontius Pilate, who sentenced Jesus to death even though Pilate thought he was innocent: "'Why? What crime has this man committed? I have found in him no grounds for the death penalty'" (*Luke 23: 22*).

Blasphemy means insulting or showing a lack of respect for God. SUPPORT

The crucifixion

Jesus was put to death by **crucifixion**, which means being nailed to a cross and left to die. He was crucified between two criminals. The sky went dark from midday until around 3pm, when he died.

> ❝Wanting to release Jesus, Pilate appealed to them again. But they kept shouting, **"Crucify him! Crucify him!"**❞
> (*Luke 23: 20–21*)

> ❝It was now about noon, and darkness came over the whole land until three in the afternoon, for the sun stopped shining. And the curtain of the temple was torn in two. Jesus called out with a loud voice, "Father, into your hands I commit my spirit." When he had said this, he breathed his last. The centurion, seeing what had happened, praised God and said, "Surely this was a righteous man."❞
> (*Luke 23: 44–47*)

For Christians, Jesus' death on the cross was proof of his humanity – he did actually die. This means that Jesus truly was God incarnate.

Christians believe Jesus' death was a sacrifice – his death brought about the forgiveness of humanity's **sins**. Through Jesus' death and resurrection, forgiveness becomes available to humanity and the loving relationship with God is restored (see 1.5).

Christians remember the crucifixion on Good Friday through worship, hymn-singing and prayers.

🔑 USEFUL TERMS

Crucifixion: being nailed to a cross and left to die

Sin: anything that prevents a relationship with God, either because the person does something they shouldn't, or neglects to do something they should

B An image from the 2004 film *The Passion of the Christ*, showing Jesus carrying the cross on which he is to be crucified

USEFUL TERMS

Ascension: going up into heaven

Resurrection: rising from the dead; also the view that after death God recreates a new body in a heavenly place

Jesus' resurrection

The Bible teaches that Jesus rose from the dead on the third day after he died. This is called the **resurrection**. For Christians, it shows that Jesus really was God and could overcome death.

A group of women went to Jesus' tomb to prepare his body for a proper burial. They discovered that the body had gone. According to the Bible, Jesus had risen:

> ❛Why do you look for the living among the dead? **He is not here; he has risen!** Remember how he told you [...] The Son of Man must be delivered over to the hands of sinners, be crucified and on the third day be raised again.❜
> *(Luke 24: 5–7)*

For Christians, this is important because it means that all Jesus taught is true. It means that humanity's sins are forgiven, people can have a true relationship with God again, and death is no longer the end. Christians believe that, if they believe in Jesus and follow his teachings, they will receive eternal life and be reunited with God. They remember the resurrection on Easter Sunday, which is a joyful celebration.

> ❛... you, with the help of wicked men, put him to death by nailing him to the cross. But **God raised him from the dead**, freeing him from the agony of death, because it was impossible for death to keep its hold on him.❜
> *(Acts 2: 23–24)*

> ❛**Christ died for our sins** according to the scriptures, that he was buried, that he was raised on the third day...❜
> *(1 Corinthians 15: 3–4)*

C According to the Bible, Jesus' tomb was found to be empty, with the large stone door rolled to one side

STRETCH

What does it mean to say that Jesus overcame death? Did Jesus die and then rise from the dead? Give reasons for your point of view. If Jesus didn't die, what do you think did happen?

Jesus' ascension

The Bible teaches that, after Jesus rose from the dead, he spent time teaching his disciples. He told them that he would soon be taken up to heaven (see 1.6) but that they would not be left alone. The Holy Spirit would come into the world and help them to spread the word of God.

> ❝ "... in a few days you will be baptised with the Holy Spirit. [...] You will receive power when the Holy Spirit comes on you; and you will be my witnesses in Jerusalem, and in all Judea and Samaria, and to the ends of the earth." After he said this, **he was taken up before their very eyes**, and a cloud hid him from their sight. ❞
>
> *(Acts 1: 5–9)*

The last sentence of this quotation describes Jesus being taken up to heaven. This is called the **ascension**. Many Christians remember the ascension on Ascension Sunday through worship, hymn-singing and prayers.

D The ascension of Jesus depicted in a stained glass window in a Nottinghamshire church

BUILD YOUR SKILLS

1   Copy and complete the following table for the four important terms from the life and death of Jesus given in this unit.

Term	What does it mean?	Why is it important for Christians?
Last Supper		
Crucifixion		
Resurrection		
Ascension		

2   Consider whether you agree or disagree with each of the following statements and explain why.
   a   'Only Christians should be allowed to celebrate Christmas.'
   b   'Easter is about the death of Jesus, not about Easter eggs.'
   c   'Jesus did not exist.'
   d   'Jesus has no importance in today's world.'

3   Read *Luke 22–24*, taking notes about the key events. What can Christians learn about Jesus from these events? Write two paragraphs and explain your reasons using quotations.   **STRETCH**

SUMMARY

- Christians believe that Jesus is both God and man. They believe he was crucified, rose from the dead and, after a short time, ascended into heaven.

- Christians claim that all who believe in Jesus can have eternal life.

- Jesus taught people how to pray and how to have a relationship with God through love and worship.

 EXAM-STYLE QUESTIONS

a   Outline **three** events in the last days of Jesus' life. (3)

d   'Jesus' crucifixion was the most important event in history.' Evaluate this statement considering arguments for and against. In your response you should:
   - refer to Christian teachings
   - reach a justified conclusion. (15)

What is salvation?

Jesus Christ came to bring what Christians call **salvation**, by saving them from their sin and reuniting them with God. The Bible says:

> ❛For God did not send his Son into the world to condemn the world, but **to save the world** through him.❜
> *(John 3: 17)*

So what does this mean? Christians believe that everyone was created for a relationship with God. Whether the account of Adam and Eve is taken as literal or not, it does show that humanity had a perfect relationship with God until they chose to walk away from it. Some Christians suggest that because Adam and Eve sinned against God, all humanity is automatically sinful and in need of salvation. Other Christians believe that people are not automatically sinful, but that all will sin at one time or another.

In many ways the nature of sin is not the primary focus of Christianity. The primary focus is on the God who loved humanity so much that he sent Jesus to die on the cross so that whoever believed in him would have a relationship with God forever *(John 3: 16)*.

SPECIFICATION FOCUS

The nature and significance of salvation and the role of Christ within salvation: law, sin, grace and Spirit, the role of Christ in salvation including John 3: 10–21 and Acts 4: 8–12; the nature and significance of atonement within Christianity and its link to salvation.

USEFUL TERMS

Atonement: the action of restoring a relationship; in Christianity, Jesus' death and resurrection restores the relationship between God and human beings

Grace: undeserved love

Law: guidelines as to how people should behave

Repentance: to say sorry for, and turn away from, any wrongdoing

Salvation: being saved from sin and the consequences of sin; going to **heaven** (see 1.6)

A A modern stained glass window in St Edmundsbury Cathedral showing an angel banishing Adam and Eve from the Garden of Eden

Law, sin, grace, and Spirit

Christians believe that people were separated from the love of God because they did wrongful things (sin) and disobeyed the **law** of God. The law consists of guidelines on how people should behave and the most famous part is the Ten Commandments (*Exodus 20*).

However, Jesus taught that the law was not enough to save people (*Matthew 5: 20*) and he was critical of those who congratulated themselves on keeping the law (*Luke 5: 32*). What was needed was **repentance** and an acceptance that righteousness was not possible without the **grace** that came through Jesus.

In other words, people might think that by trying really hard to be good they can achieve God's favour, but this is not the case in the Christian faith. In the Book of Acts, the Apostle Peter explains that the only way that people can be saved is through Jesus:

> ❝ **Salvation is found in no one else**, for there is no other name under heaven given to mankind by which we must be saved. ❞
> (*Acts 4: 12*)

Christians therefore believe that they must turn away from sin, receive the freely given gift of grace through Jesus, and have faith in him, in order to be saved. Christians believe that, when they make this decision for the first time, they also welcome the Holy Spirit into their lives.

B *Christ of Saint John of the Cross by Salvador Dalí (1951)*

What is atonement?

Christians believe that, because Jesus died to save humanity from sin, the relationship between God and humanity was restored. This is called **atonement** or, more literally, 'at-one-ment'. God and humans are 'at one' because of Jesus.

Christians believe Jesus died as an act of love to save humanity, even though humanity did not deserve it. His love is called grace, which means undeserved love.

Use this diagram and the information on this page to explain what **atonement** means in your own words.

SUPPORT

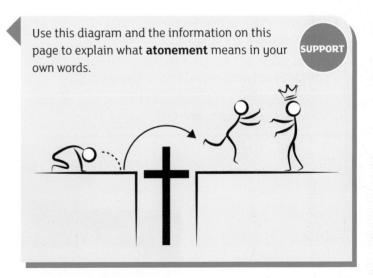

What is the significance of atonement and salvation within Christianity?

- Christians believe Jesus' death allows humans to have eternal life.
- Christians have a moral duty to live their lives as Jesus lived his, loving and caring for each other: 'I have set you an example that you should do as I have done for you.' (*John 13: 15*). In this way, humans are saved from the power and consequences of sin.
- God and humanity can have their loving relationship restored. Christians regularly repent of any wrongdoing and believe that, because of Jesus, they are forgiven by God.

BUILD YOUR SKILLS

1 Complete the following table concerning salvation:

Term	What does it mean?	Why is it important for Christians?
Sin		
Salvation		
Sacrifice		
Atonement		

2 Read through this topic carefully and write an answer to each of the following questions, making sure you explain your points:
   a Why did the Son of God come to earth as a human?
   b Why doesn't God just forgive sins?
   c Do you believe humans need the salvation that Jesus offers?
   d How does atonement link to salvation?

EXAM-STYLE QUESTIONS

a Outline **three** features of salvation for Christians. (3)

c Explain **two** reasons why salvation is important for Christians today. In your answer you must refer to a source of wisdom and authority. (5)

SUMMARY

- Christians believe that Jesus came to save humanity from the consequences of sin; this is called salvation.
- Jesus' death and resurrection brought about atonement – making humanity and God 'at one' again.
- Christians believe that, because of Jesus, they are able to have a relationship with God.

C Christians pray regularly to repent of their wrongdoings and to receive forgiveness from God

1.6 Christian eschatology

Eschatology is an area of Christian teaching which is all about life after death. All living things eventually die, but Christians believe that there is another life beyond this physical life. Here are a few Christian beliefs.

> When we die, the souls of the good go to a wonderful paradise called **heaven** to be with God.

> When we die, the souls of the wicked go to a place of eternal punishment called **hell**.

> On the Last Day, God will raise the dead in bodily form. This is resurrection.

The Bible teaches that all who believe in Jesus will have eternal life:

> ' For God so loved the world that he gave his one and only Son, that **whoever believes in him shall not perish but have eternal life**. '
> *(John 3: 16)*

Christians think of life after death in divergent ways:

- The most common view is that everyone has an **immortal soul** that leaves our physical body when we die and goes to God in heaven, or otherwise goes to hell. This view holds that followers of Jesus who die will go to heaven and those who are not followers of Jesus will go to hell. Christians differ on what they think heaven and hell will be like.

- Some Christians believe that Jesus died to forgive all sins, and so everyone (not just Christians) will live forever in heaven. This is called **universalism**.

- Many Catholics believe in **purgatory**, where the dead are purified of their sins before going to heaven.

Christians also vary on whether the above happens as soon as people die, or at the end of time, on what Christians call the **Day of Judgement**.

Heaven

Heaven is the place where Christians believe that they will spend the afterlife. It is not described in detail in the Bible, so Christians have different views about what it will be like. Some believe that it is a physical place, whilst others believe it is a state of being spiritually united with God. The Bible teaches that heaven is a place of everlasting peace and joy for those who believe in Jesus:

> ' Then I saw "a new heaven and a new earth" [...] I saw the Holy City, the new Jerusalem, coming down out of heaven from God [...] He will wipe every tear from their eyes. There will be no more death or mourning or crying or pain... '
> *(Revelation 21: 1–4)*

SPECIFICATION FOCUS

Christian eschatology: divergent Christian teachings about life after death, including the nature and significance of resurrection, judgement, heaven, and hell and purgatory with reference to the 39 Articles of Religion and Catholic teachings; how beliefs about life after death are shown in the Bible, including reference to 2 Corinthians 5: 1–10 and divergent understandings as to why they are important for Christians today.

USEFUL TERMS

Day of Judgement: time when God assesses a person's life and actions

Eschatology: an area of Christian theology which is concerned with life after death

Heaven: place of eternal paradise where Christians believe they will spend the afterlife

Hell: place of punishment and separation from God

Immortal soul: a soul that lives on after the death of the physical body

Purgatory: a place where the souls of the dead are cleansed and prepared for heaven

Universalism: the belief that because of the love and mercy of God everyone will go to heaven

A

Hell

Many Christians believe in hell, a place of punishment and separation from God. Some Christians do not believe in hell, and instead believe that those who are not followers of Jesus would simply cease to exist when they die. Like heaven, the descriptions of hell in the Bible are not detailed:

> ❛He will punish those who do not know God and do not obey the gospel of our Lord Jesus. They will be punished with everlasting destruction...❜
> *(2 Thessalonians 1: 8–9)*

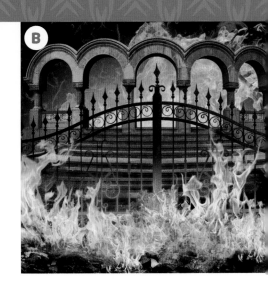

Purgatory

Purgatory, from the Latin word *purgare* meaning 'make clean', is a concept mainly associated with the Catholic Church. It is a place (or state of mind) where the souls of those who have died go to be purified until they are made clean from their sins and can then go to heaven. The *Catechism of the Catholic Church* describes it in this way:

> ❛All who die in God's grace and friendship, but still imperfectly purified, are indeed assured of their eternal salvation; but **after death they undergo purification**, so as to achieve the holiness necessary to enter the joy of heaven.❜
> *Catechism of the Catholic Church, 1030*

However, this is not a view held by Protestant Christians. The *39 Articles of Religion*, which is an ancient statement of the beliefs and teachings of the Church of England, says the following about purgatory:

> ❛The Romish Doctrine concerning Purgatory [...] is a fond thing vainly invented, and grounded upon no warranty of Scripture, but rather repugnant to the Word of God.❜
> *(Article 22, 39 Articles of Religion)*

This is a strongly worded criticism of the idea of purgatory:
- '**Fond thing vainly invented**' means they believe it has been made up
- '**Grounded upon no warranty of Scripture**' means they don't believe it is backed up by the Bible
- '**Repugnant**' means unacceptable.

Judgement

Christians believe that God is just, fair and merciful. They believe in the Day of Judgement, when God will judge all people according to how they lived their lives on earth and to give them the afterlife they deserve.

> ❛And I saw the dead, great and small, standing before the throne [...] the dead were judged according to what they had done...❜
> *(Revelation 20: 12)*

Christians also believe in the Second Coming, when Jesus will return to earth. This will be the time for judgement and the establishment of God's kingdom.

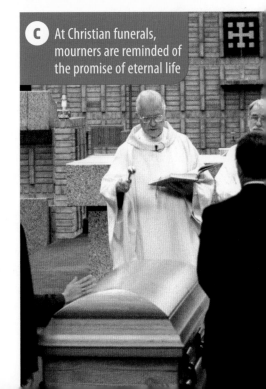

C At Christian funerals, mourners are reminded of the promise of eternal life

Resurrection

For Christians, the resurrection of Jesus has made sure that there will be an afterlife for all who believe in him. In *1 Corinthians 15: 12*, St Paul wrote, 'But if it is preached that Christ has been raised from the dead, how can some of you say that there is no resurrection of the dead?' Paul argues that if Christians believe that Jesus rose from the dead, then they must believe they can look forward to an afterlife.

Therefore, many Christians believe that, at the end of time, God will raise their bodies to life again, as he did with Jesus' body. The appearances of Jesus after his resurrection are usually thought by Christians to be the strongest evidence that this will happen. According to the Bible, when Jesus appeared to his disciples after death they were able to touch him (*Luke 24: 39*). Paul uses the metaphor of buildings to explain what will happen to the body after death:

> What do you think Paul means by saying that because Jesus rose from the dead they can have an afterlife? **STRETCH**

> ❝ For we know that if the earthly tent we live in is destroyed, we have a building from God, an eternal house in heaven, not built by human hands. ❞
> *(2 Corinthians 5: 1)*

In other words, the physical human body eventually dies, but a resurrected body goes on forever.

Why is life after death important for Christians today?

- Jesus said that those who believe in him would have life after death.
- Life after death is a reward for faithful people.
- Life after death offers hope for the future.
- Life after death allows Christians to be with God forever.

COMPARE AND CONTRAST

In your exam, you could be asked to **compare and contrast** Christian beliefs on life after death with the beliefs of another religion you are studying. You should consider the similarities and differences between them.

BUILD YOUR SKILLS

1 Look at images **A** and **B**. How successful are they at depicting heaven and hell? Explain your reasons and refer to Christian beliefs.

2 Here are some divergent views about life after death.
- 'If God really loves us, everyone should go to heaven.'
- 'There is no life after death. When we die, we just die.'
- 'People who are bad should go to hell as a punishment.'
- a Consider whether you agree or disagree with each statement and explain why.
- b How might a religious believer respond to each statement?

EXAM-STYLE QUESTIONS

b Describe **two** differences between Christian beliefs on life after death and those of another religion you have studied. (4)
d 'There is no life after death.' Evaluate this statement considering arguments for and against. In your response you should:
- refer to Christian teachings
- refer to different Christian points of view
- reach a justified conclusion. (15)

SUMMARY

- Christian belief in the afterlife is very important and is connected to beliefs about Jesus' own death and resurrection and what that means for Christians.
- There are divergent views within Christianity about the nature of heaven and hell, purgatory, and the resurrection of the body.

What is God like?

There are two characteristics of God's nature that are particularly important in helping Christians to approach the problem of evil and suffering:

- **Omnipotence** – God is all-powerful
- **Benevolence** – God is all-good/loving.

Christians believe that, if God is all-powerful, then nothing is impossible for him; if he is all-good, then he is loving and cannot do wrong. In the Bible, God's love and power means that he not only *wants* to help people, but he is also *able* to:

> ❛The Lord works righteousness and justice for all the oppressed❜
> *(Psalm 103: 6)*

What is the problem of evil and suffering?

Evil is the opposite of good: it causes pain, grief and damage. Evil and suffering can be on a large scale or a smaller, personal scale, as almost everyone experiences pain and suffering at different times in their lives.

There are two types of evil and suffering:

- **Natural evil**: suffering caused by nature that is beyond human control.
- **Moral evil**: deliberately evil actions by human beings that cause suffering to others.

🔍 **SPECIFICATION FOCUS**

The problem of evil/suffering and a loving and righteous God: the problems it raises for Christians about the nature of God, including reference to omnipotence and benevolence, including Psalm 103; how the problem may cause believers to question their faith or the existence of God; the nature and examples of natural suffering, moral suffering.

🔑 **USEFUL TERMS**

Benevolence: all-good

Moral evil: suffering caused by humans, such as war

Natural evil: suffering caused by natural events, such as earthquakes

Omnipotence: all-powerful

A Examples of natural evil; image shows a man rescuing an unknown girl from flood waters in Bangkok

Earthquakes

Disease

Famine

Volcanoes

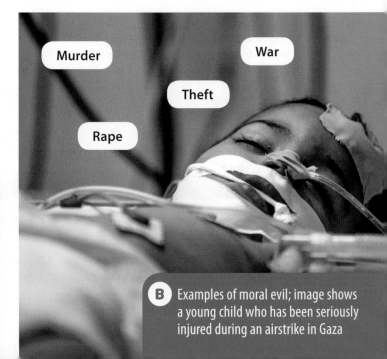

B Examples of moral evil; image shows a young child who has been seriously injured during an airstrike in Gaza

Murder

War

Theft

Rape

How might the problem lead some people to question God's existence?

The existence of evil and suffering in the world is one of the strongest arguments against the existence of God. If it is true that God is all-powerful and all-loving, it seems logical that he should prevent evil and suffering. Since evil and suffering *do* exist, some people have concluded that God does *not*.

The problem can be expressed in this way:

- God is thought to be all-loving (benevolent) and all-powerful (omnipotent).
- If God is benevolent he would *want* to remove evil and suffering.
- If God is omnipotent he would *be able* to remove evil and suffering.
- Therefore, both God and evil cannot exist together, yet evil *does* exist.
- Therefore, God cannot exist.

This can be illustrated in the form of an inconsistent triad (see image **C**).

C The inconsistent triad; if you combine any two points of the triangle, the third point is disproved

Why does the problem cause believers to question their faith?

The problem of evil challenges the existence and characteristics of God. This can cause believers to doubt their beliefs, especially if they or their loved ones are experiencing pain. In times of doubt, a Christian might ask:

- If God exists but isn't all-powerful and all-loving, how can I worship him?
- If God is not all-powerful or not all-loving, is that a God I want to believe in?
- If God is all-powerful and all-loving, how could he allow suffering?

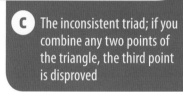

Many people find it difficult to understand what it means to say that God is all-loving. Some believe God should only love those who are good. If God is all-loving, does he love tyrants and mass murderers? **SUPPORT**

BUILD YOUR SKILLS

1 What are the two kinds of evil? Can you give five examples of each kind? **SUPPORT**

2 Write down a potential problem of God's omnipotence.
   a How would a non-religious person respond?
   b How would a Christian respond?

3 a Is a God who is not all-powerful still worthy of a Christian's worship? Why/why not? **STRETCH**
   b If God is benevolent, can he ever be bad?

SUMMARY

- Christians believe that God is omnipotent and benevolent.
- There are two types of evil in the world: natural evil and moral evil.
- Some people question whether the existence of evil and suffering shows that God either does not exist or is not all-powerful or all-loving.

EXAM-STYLE QUESTIONS

a Outline **three** features of the problem of evil and suffering. (3)
b Explain **two** types of evil and suffering. (4)

1.8 Divergent solutions to the problem of evil

Biblical solutions

In the Bible there are many references to evil and suffering, and suggestions that suffering is part of life. This is sometimes linked to the existence of a personal force of evil, given different names in the history of Christianity: the Devil, **Satan** or Lucifer. In Christianity, Satan (which means 'the adversary') was one of God's angels who had rebelled against the rule of God. In the Book of Job, a good man and a believer in God suffers great hardship and tragedy after God is challenged by Satan.

> **❛** What I feared has come upon me;
> **what I dreaded has happened to me.**
> I have no peace, no quietness.
> I have no rest, but only turmoil. **❜**
> *(Job 3: 25–26)*

In the midst of Job's suffering, God tells him that the problem of evil and suffering has no simple answer and that he must trust God. In the end, all turns out well for Job.

> **❛** The fear of the Lord – that is wisdom,
> and to shun evil is understanding. **❜**
> *(Job 28: 28)*

> **❛** I know that you [God] can do all things;
> no purpose of yours can be thwarted. **❜**
> *(Job 42: 2)*

SPECIFICATION FOCUS

Divergent solutions offered to the problem of evil/suffering and a loving and righteous God: biblical, theoretical and practical, including reference to Psalm 119, Job, free will, vale of soul-making, prayer, and charity; the success of solutions to the problem.

USEFUL TERMS

Satan: 'the adversary'; one of God's angels who rebelled against the rule of God

STRETCH

The story of Job is very complex and raises questions. If God is all-powerful, why does he allow Satan to tell him what to do or exist at all? If God is all-loving, why does he permit the suffering of a good man? The answer seems to be that God is mysterious and humans are not allowed to know everything. What do you think?

A This child has no parents and no home, and has to beg on the streets of Mumbai in order to survive. For some people, the question of why suffering happens has no easy answer.

The Book of Psalms is a collection of songs and prayers dedicated to God in which the theme of suffering is very common. Some of the psalms express feelings of abandonment by God:

> ❛Save me, O God, for the waters have come up to my neck. [...] I am worn out calling for help; my throat is parched. **My eyes fail, looking for my God.** ❜
> *(Psalm 69: 1, 3)*

Psalm 119 acknowledges the existence of suffering as part of life, but also states that God is trustworthy:

> ❛My comfort in my suffering is this: Your promise preserves my life. ❜
> *(Psalm 119: 50)*

> ❛My soul faints with longing for your salvation, but I have put my hope in your word. ❜
> *(Psalm 119: 81)*

Other psalms praise God for his help in times of trouble:

> ❛**I called to the Lord**, who is worthy of praise,
> **and I have been saved** from my enemies. ❜
> *(Psalm 18: 3)*

The Bible teaches that, one day, God will end all evil and suffering for good:

> ❛**He will wipe every tear from their eyes**. There will be no more death or mourning or crying or pain, for the old order of things has passed away. ❜
> *(Revelation 21: 4)*

Biblical solutions to evil and suffering encourage Christians to believe:

- Suffering is part of life.
- Christians can pray to God to get comfort in their suffering and they should praise God for his help in times of trouble.
- God is love, but sometimes it's hard to understand why God doesn't intervene. Faith sometimes involves trust without understanding.
- One day all suffering will come to an end.

B A mother and child light a candle in an Orthodox church; many Christians light candles when they pray as a symbol of Jesus bringing hope in times of darkness

Theoretical solutions

Christians may respond by looking at what is behind the problem and how it may be resolved. In the Bible, *Genesis 2–3* highlights this very clearly by showing that evil and suffering can be the result of human free will. The first human beings, Adam and Eve, used their free will to disobey God. When they did so, evil and suffering were brought into the world and they were separated from God.

> ❝So the Lord God banished him [Adam] from the garden of Eden to work the ground from which he had been taken.❞
> *(Genesis 3: 23)*

Some Christians go further and say that this world is a **vale of soul-making** – an environment where everything that is necessary for human growth and development can be found. For instance, in the midst of evil and suffering there are opportunities to do good, or to do bad, to choose the right way or the wrong way.

> Theoretical solutions to evil and suffering encourage Christians to believe:
> - God gives humans free will to act as they wish.
> - Humans may choose to do evil or inflict suffering and that's why evil exists.
> - Suffering helps people to develop good characteristics.

Practical responses

Christians believe that suffering is part of life, and they have a duty to respond to this practically:

- They can develop positive qualities such as compassion and kindness, courage and honesty.
- They can help each other to make the world a better place and learn how to improve things for themselves and future generations.
- They can help through involvement in charity work.
- They can pray for God's help and encouragement.

Many Christians pray for those who are suffering. This is called **intercession**. They believe that they can change the impacts of evil and suffering by praying to God on behalf of those who are suffering.

> Practical responses to evil and suffering encourage Christians to believe:
> - Christians can develop positive qualities such as compassion.
> - Suffering is part of life but help can be given.
> - Christians can help by praying and doing charitable work.

🔑 USEFUL TERMS

Intercession: prayers for those who are suffering

Vale of soul-making: an environment in which human beings can overcome evil by making good choices

---

Some Christians say that the world provides all they need to choose to be good or bad people. Can you think of some examples? **SUPPORT**

C Many Christians meet together to pray in times of difficulty

The success of solutions to the problem

	Strengths	Weaknesses
Biblical solutions	• Help Christians to understand God more clearly and trust that he will make everything right in the end. • Help Christians to believe that God acts for good in the world.	• People in the Bible still experience suffering, and God does not always stop it. • It can be harder to trust God when things aren't going well.
Theoretical solutions	• Explain that evil and suffering come from human free will, not from God. • Encourage Christians to use times of evil and suffering to make the right choices and grow closer to God.	• God created the universe, therefore he must be responsible for the existence of evil. • It may not be reasonable to expect people to respond well in times of suffering.
Practical responses	Christians would say that practical responses to evil and suffering are not a 'solution' to the problem, but they can be successful in easing suffering. Christians believe suffering is a reality of life, and they have a choice to respond practically to help with the consequences.	

BUILD YOUR SKILLS

1 Of the solutions to the problem of evil and suffering,
   a which is the most successful?
   b which is the least successful?
   Give your reasons.

2 Would the world be a better place if there was no evil and suffering? Discuss with a partner.

3 Look through a newspaper and make a list of all the news stories involving suffering. Then answer these questions: **STRETCH**
   a What was the suffering shown in each incident?
   b Was the suffering in each case an act of nature or caused by human actions?
   c How could the suffering in each case have been prevented?
   d Do you think that prayer would be useful in these situations? Think carefully about what you think prayer accomplishes.

SUMMARY

• The problem of evil and suffering challenges the existence of God because if God is all-good and all-powerful, why doesn't he put an end to suffering?

• Christians respond to evil and suffering in different ways, including reading the Bible, praying, and working to relieve suffering.

• Christians might argue that God gave humans free will, and that evil and suffering are the consequences of human action.

EXAM-STYLE QUESTIONS

c Explain **two** different Christian solutions to the problem of evil and suffering. In your answer you must refer to a source of wisdom and authority. (5)

d 'God is not responsible for suffering in the world.' Evaluate this statement considering arguments for and against. In your response you should:
   • refer to Christian teachings
   • refer to different Christian points of view
   • reach a justified conclusion. (15)

Revision

BUILD YOUR SKILLS

Look at the list of 'I can' statements below and think carefully about how confident you are. Use the following code to rate each of the statements. Be honest!

Green – very confident. What is your evidence for this?

Orange – quite confident. What is your target? Be specific.

Red – not confident. What is your target? Be specific.

A self-assessment revision checklist is available on *Kerboodle*

I can...

- Explain what the Trinity is and why the oneness of God is significant

- Give reasons why the Trinity is significant in Christianity

- Give quotations from the Bible and the Nicene Creed about the Trinity

- Explain the characteristics of the Trinity – Father, Son, and Holy Spirit

- Describe how the Trinity is reflected in Christian worship and belief today

- Describe the biblical account of creation

- Explain two different ways that Christians interpret creation

- Explain the role of the Word and Spirit in creation with reference to sources of wisdom and authority

- Explain the importance of creation for Christians today

- Explain the meaning of the incarnation with reference to a source of wisdom and authority

- Explain why the incarnation is so important to Christians

- Describe the key events in the last days of Jesus' life (including the Last Supper, betrayal, arrest, trial, crucifixion, resurrection and ascension of Jesus), with reference to the accounts of these within the Bible

- Give reasons why these events are significant, and describe what they show about the person of Jesus

- Explain the idea of salvation and why it is so important within Christianity

- Explain the role of Jesus in salvation including reference to a source of wisdom and authority

- Define atonement, and explain how it links to salvation

- Explain different Christian views on life after death

- Explain the meaning and significance of resurrection, judgement, heaven, hell, and purgatory with reference to sources of wisdom and authority

- Describe the problem of evil and suffering, with reference to natural and moral evil

- Explain the problems suffering raises for Christians about the nature of God

- Explain how evil and suffering can challenge religious belief

- Describe different solutions to the problem of evil and suffering, including biblical, theoretical and practical solutions

- Discuss the success of the solutions to the problem of evil.

Exam practice

On these exam practice pages you will see example answers for each of the exam question types: **a**, **b**, **c**, and **d**. You can find out more about these on pages 6–11.

• Question 'a'

*Question **a** is AO1 – this tests your knowledge and understanding.*

> (a) Outline **three** features of the biblical story of creation. (3)

Student response

God created the earth in six days and then he rested.

 WHAT WENT WELL

This student has correctly identified an aspect of the biblical story of creation.

Improved student response

The biblical story of creation says that God is the creator. He created the earth in six days and then rested. He looked at his creation and decided that it was good.

 Over to you! Give yourself three minutes on the clock and have a go at answering this question. Remember, this question type requires you to provide three facts or short ideas: you don't need to explain them or express any opinions.

 HOW TO IMPROVE

This answer does not outline three features of the biblical story of creation. For a high level response, three distinct features should be given. See the 'improved student response' opposite for suggested corrections.

• Question 'b'

*Question **b** is AO1 – this tests your knowledge and understanding.*

> (a) Explain **two** Christian beliefs about the incarnation. (4)

Student response

The Son of God came to earth, and he was born a human called Jesus.

 WHAT WENT WELL

The student has given a correct Christian belief and explained it.

Improved student response

The incarnation is a core Christian doctrine which holds that the Son of God came to earth, and he was born a human called Jesus.

Christians also believe that the incarnation took place for a special purpose, which was to restore the relationship between God and humanity which had been destroyed by sin.

 Over to you! Give yourself four minutes on the clock and have a go at answering this question. Remember, in order to 'explain' something, you need to **develop** your points. See page 9 for a reminder of how to do this.

 HOW TO IMPROVE

The question asks for two Christian beliefs about the incarnation, and the answer only contains one. For a high level response, students should explain two Christian beliefs about the incarnation. See the 'improved student response' opposite for suggested corrections.

• Question 'c'

*Question **c** is AO1 – this tests your knowledge and understanding.*

> (c) Explain **two** different Christian beliefs about life after death. In your answer you must refer to a source of wisdom and authority. (5)

Student response

Roman Catholic Christians believe in the existence of purgatory, a place where the souls of the dead go to be purified after death. This is so that they can achieve holiness before entering heaven.

The Church of England does not believe in the existence of purgatory however, and argues that it is not referred to in the Bible.

Improved student response

Roman Catholic Christians believe in the existence of purgatory, a place where the souls of the dead go to be purified after death. This is so that they can achieve holiness before entering heaven.

The Church of England does not believe in the existence of purgatory however, and argues that it is not referred to in the Bible. The 39 Articles of Religion claim that it has been 'invented' (Article 22).

 Over to you! Give yourself five minutes on the clock and have a go at answering this question. Remember, you need to write two developed points, one of which needs to be supported by a source of wisdom and authority.

 WHAT WENT WELL

This student has correctly explained two different Christian beliefs about life after death.

 HOW TO IMPROVE

The student hasn't referred to a source of wisdom and authority. See the 'improved student response' opposite for a suggested correction.

• Question 'd'

*Question **d** is AO2 – this tests your ability to evaluate. Some 'd' questions also carry an extra three marks for spelling, punctuation and grammar.*

> **In this question, 3 of the marks awarded will be for your spelling, punctuation and grammar and your use of specialist terminology.**
>
> *(d) 'Christianity provides no solutions to the problem of evil and suffering.' Evaluate this statement considering arguments for and against. In your response you should:
> • refer to Christian teachings
> • refer to different Christian points of view
> • reach a justified conclusion. (15)

Student response

If God was benevolent he would not let us suffer. Christians will teach that God knows why people suffer, consequently he uses suffering to show his love and faithfulness to people and this should give them faith.

The Catholic Church teaches that it is a Christian responsibility to respond in practical ways to ease the suffering of others. Because of this many Christians will choose jobs which show they care and help other people.

However some Christians could argue that evil and suffering has nothing to do with God as in the Bible it says evil is a result of the actions of Adam and Eve. Therefore it is not a Christian's duty to provide solutions for the problem of evil and suffering.

Improved student response

For many Christians, the way they respond to suffering is a very important part of their faith. They believe that suffering brings them closer to God as <u>Christians</u> will teach that God knows why people suffer, consequently he uses suffering to show his love and faithfulness to his followers. It could be argued, however, that the existence of evil and suffering in the world challenges the claim that Christianity has anything to offer, because the problem is yet to be solved.

In contrast to this view, the existence of evil and suffering is seen by many as proof that Christians have a duty to help each other and relieve suffering in whichever way is needed. The Catholic Church teaches that it is a Christian responsibility to respond in practical ways to ease the suffering of others through charitable actions. Because of this many Christians will choose jobs which show they care and want to help other people.

However, some Christians think that the problem of evil and suffering is a direct result of the misuse of human free will and therefore has nothing to do with God. The story of the Fall places responsibility for suffering on humanity: "Cursed is the ground because of you" (Genesis 3: 17), which suggests that it is the responsibility of humans to find solutions to reducing suffering in the world.

On balance, it seems to me that the Christian faith does have solutions to offer. Salvation can only be achieved if Christians consider their actions and how they support others and this is most evident when faced with suffering.

Over to you! Give yourself 15 minutes on the clock and have a go at answering this question. Remember to refer back to the original statement in your writing when you give different points of view, and make sure you cover each of the bullet points given in the question. Allow three minutes to check your spelling, punctuation and grammar and use of specialist terminology.

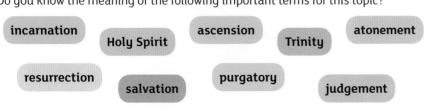

BUILD YOUR SKILLS

In your exams, you'll need to make sure you use religious terminology correctly. Do you know the meaning of the following important terms for this topic?

incarnation · Holy Spirit · ascension · Trinity · atonement · resurrection · salvation · purgatory · judgement

 WHAT WENT WELL

This is a low level response. The student understands that they must explain different Christian viewpoints.

 HOW TO IMPROVE

Both sides of this argument lack detailed understanding, and there aren't any clear links back to the question. It could be improved with a more logical chain of reasoning, and more detail, including specific references to sources of wisdom and authority. There is also a spelling error. See the 'improved student response' opposite for suggested corrections.

Chapter 2:
Crime and Punishment

COMMUNITY PAYBACK

What is justice?

In the UK, the government makes **laws** which everyone must follow. These laws must be applied in a fair and reasonable way to everyone. **Justice** means doing what is right and fair based on the law.

The criminal justice system is the system of enforcing the law. It involves arresting, prosecuting, defending, sentencing, and **punishing** people who are suspected or convicted of carrying out criminal offences. If a person is found guilty, their punishment should be in proportion to the crime they have committed.

If the law was not upheld with justice, people would stop respecting it and the government would lose its authority.

If people think that a new law is wrong or unjust, they can protest and try to influence a change by organising petitions or holding demonstrations. Demonstrations are usually peaceful, but in some cases they can become violent.

A Rioting at a demonstration against the Poll Tax in 1990, a new tax law which many people believed disadvantaged the poor

Why is justice important for Christians?

Justice is a very important principle in Christianity, because Christians believe that God is just, and requires his people to act justly too.

> ❛And what does the Lord require of you? **To act justly and to love mercy** and to walk humbly with your God.❜
> *(Micah 6: 8)*

Christians therefore support systems that uphold justice and will often speak out about situations they feel to be unjust for individuals or communities.

SPECIFICATION FOCUS

Christian attitudes towards justice: the nature of justice and why justice is important for Christians, including Micah 3 and 6; Christian responses to why justice is important for victims; non-religious attitudes (including atheist and Humanist) about why justice is important, regardless of religion and belief, and Christian responses to these attitudes.

Protest is legal in the UK. However, in many countries any form of public protest is illegal. What are the advantages and disadvantages of having the right to protest?

STRETCH

B This statue of Lady Justice stands above the Central Criminal Courts (known as the Old Bailey) in London. What does it symbolise?

The Bible has a strong emphasis on justice. The first five books of the Old Testament are often referred to by Christian scholars as 'the Law', because they contain laws given by God to humanity – among them the Ten Commandments (*Exodus 20*). Some of the laws in the UK can have their origins traced back to the laws in the Old Testament.

The Bible presents God as the ultimate judge, who will judge all people fairly:

> ❝Each person was judged according to what they had done.❞
> *(Revelation 20: 13)*

Elsewhere in the Old Testament, God warns that those in authority must rule with fairness and justice, otherwise society will collapse:

> ❝Listen, **you leaders [...] should you not embrace justice**, you who hate good and love evil [...] you rulers of Israel, who despise justice and distort all that is right; [...] Jerusalem will become a heap of rubble.❞
> *(Micah 3: 1, 2, 9, 12)*

In the New Testament, Jesus taught that simply obeying the laws of God was not enough to save people (see 1.5). He emphasised grace (undeserved love), forgiveness, and **reconciliation**. He taught that it was not for people to judge and punish each other, but they should forgive those who have done them wrong:

> ❝Do not judge, and you will not be judged. Do not condemn, and you will not be condemned. Forgive, and you will be forgiven.❞
> *(Luke 6: 37)*

Therefore, justice in Christianity is not only about punishment, but also about mercy. Christians believe that, because God is just, he will forgive people who are truly sorry for what they have done and genuinely want to change their behaviour.

> ❝Forgive us our sins, for we also forgive everyone who sins against us.❞
> *(Luke 11: 4)*

Justice is important to Christians because:

- God is just, so Christians believe they should therefore act justly too.
- The Bible has a strong emphasis on justice and contains the laws of God given to humanity.
- God is the ultimate judge who will judge all people fairly.
- God's justice, made clear through Jesus, is about forgiveness and mercy, with the aim of restoring relationships.

STRETCH

As written in *Romans 13: 1–7*, God wants Christians to obey the laws of the land they live in. But what about situations that are within these laws, but go against laws set out in the Bible? Can you find out any examples? What do you think Christians do in these situations?

SUPPORT

Is it possible to forgive every type of wrongdoing?

USEFUL TERMS

Justice: doing what is right and fair based on the law

Law: guidelines as to how people should behave; the rules that govern society

Punish: impose a penalty on someone for doing something wrong

Reconciliation: restoring peace and friendship between individuals or groups

Justice for victims: What is the Christian view?

Justice is important for victims of crime because:

- They can be reassured that the person who has hurt them will be punished fairly for what they have done.
- They may feel comfort that the person who has hurt them will not be able to hurt anyone else in the same way.
- It is an important step in achieving closure – in other words, in allowing them to move on from what has happened to them.

Christians are taught to support those who have experienced injustice, and particularly those who do not have a voice in society:

> ❝Learn to do right; seek justice. **Defend the oppressed.** Take up the cause of the fatherless; plead the case of the widow.❞
> *(Isaiah 1: 17)*

For Christians, defending the oppressed involves standing up for those who are unable to stand up for themselves. For example, Christian organisations such as Churches Together are active in seeking justice for victims of domestic violence.

For Christians who are victims themselves, there are key principles that they would seek to follow. The Bible teaches that they should avoid seeking revenge, as this can corrupt them. Instead, people should overcome evil with good, by trying to bless those who are at fault and forgive them. All the while, they can trust that God will avenge them justly (*Romans 12: 14–21*).

C *The Return of the Prodigal Son*, by Rembrandt (1668); this painting shows a scene from Jesus' famous parable in which a father forgives his son (*Luke 15: 11–32*)

D *God Judging Adam*, by William Blake (1795)

Why is justice important to non-religious people?

Justice is important to non-religious people for the same reasons it is important in society: it maintains peace and order, it ensures that everyone is treated fairly according to their actions, and it ensures victims obtain the justice they deserve.

Atheists do not believe in God, and **agnostics** do not believe it is possible to know whether or not God exists. Therefore, people who would define themselves in these ways would not consult any higher power when it comes to justice. They would disagree with the Christian view that God is the ultimate judge, and would instead support a fair justice system.

Non-religious people, particularly **Humanists**, would also abide by the 'Golden Rule' as an important principle, which is: 'do as you would have others do to you'. People should be treated with respect – not only victims, but also criminals; they should receive a fair trial, be allowed to defend themselves, and be treated humanely while in custody. Another key Humanist principle is that people are free to act however they wish, as long as it does not cause harm to others. When others are harmed, justice is needed in order to protect society.

Christian responses

Christians and non-religious people alike support justice and many religious and non-religious organisations work to support victims of crime. The most important difference is that non-religious people do not believe that God is an agent of justice, do not behave according to laws set out in the Bible, and do not believe in an afterlife in which they will be punished or rewarded.

Christians would argue that God is real and is active in defending them. They would argue that core Christian principles, such as forgiveness and reconciliation, are given special meaning through Jesus. They believe Jesus enables all people who truly repent of wrongdoing to be forgiven by God. This does not mean that they do not need to serve justice in this life, but they are not prevented from being united with God in this life or the life to come.

BUILD YOUR SKILLS

1   What does justice mean, and why is it important in society?

2   Look at images **C** and **D**. Using the Christian teachings described in this topic, answer the following:
   a   What aspects of Christian justice are represented in image **C**?
   b   What aspects of Christian justice are represented in image **D**?
   c   Are these two approaches compatible? Explain your reasons, referring to Christian points of view.

3   'Belief in God makes no difference to justice in this world.' List arguments for and against this statement, including non-religious and Christian perspectives.

USEFUL TERMS

Agnostic: someone who believes it is not possible to know whether or not God exists

Atheist: someone who does not believe in the existence of God

Humanist: a non-religious person who looks to reason and empathy in order to live a meaningful life

SUMMARY

- Law and justice are vital to the smooth running of society.
- Christians believe that God is just and requires people to act justly.
- The Bible teaches Christians to support victims of crime.
- Justice is also important to non-religious people, who apply principles such as the 'Golden Rule'.

EXAM-STYLE QUESTIONS

a   Outline **three** Christian beliefs about justice. (3)
b   Explain **two** Christian responses to why justice is important for victims. (4)

What is crime and what problems can it cause?

A crime is an action that is against the law and which may result in punishment. The law is enforced by the police and the courts.

We need laws so that:

- everyone is protected from crime and can live without fear
- people and their possessions are kept safe
- people know how to act towards each other.

Crime causes hurt to individuals and communities, and if it is not punished or if it is unfairly punished, it can threaten peace and stability in society. Those who commit crime are not abiding by the rules of society; these rules have been devised for the protection of people and the world in which they live.

Types of crime

The most common crimes that occur in the UK are:

- theft
- violence
- criminal damage (damaging property)
- public order offences (e.g. disturbing the peace; causing fear).

Other less common but serious crimes include:

- murder
- sexual offences
- drug offences
- possession of weapons.

Causes of crime

There is much research into the possible causes of crime. Factors that may be involved include:

- **poverty:** people may turn to crime if they have no job, house, or money, and they may feel angry at their lack of income and opportunity
- **social environment:** factors such as family dysfunction and the influence of friends and relatives may lead people to become involved in crime
- **addiction:** people may resort to criminal acts to fund their addiction to alcohol or drugs
- **hate:** sometimes people commit criminal acts out of hate, for example because of prejudice in relation to a person's race, gender, or sexuality
- **mental illness:** people may sometimes commit crimes if their judgement and behaviour are affected by mental health problems

 SPECIFICATION FOCUS

Christian attitudes towards crime: Christian teachings and responses to the nature, causes and problem of crime; Christian teachings about crime, including John 8: 1–11; what action is taken by Christian individuals and Christian groups to end crime, including Prison Fellowship and Street Pastors.

Theft can include burglary, robbery, shoplifting, theft from vehicles, fraud, and some forms of **cybercrime**. **SUPPORT**

 USEFUL TERMS

Adultery: a couple having sex even though one (or both) of them is married to someone else

Civil disobedience: refusing to comply with certain laws as a peaceful form of protest against them

Cybercrime: crime committed online

- **civil disobedience:** people may sometimes choose to disobey laws that they think are unfair
- **boredom:** some people commit crimes because they have nothing better to do; this has often been cited as the reason young people steal cars.

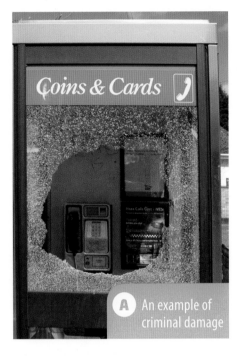

A An example of criminal damage

B Some crimes are extremely serious

C Cybercrime is a modern type of crime that can take many forms

What are Christian teachings about crime?

Christianity teaches that people should obey the law of the land in which they live:

> ❛Let everyone be subject to the governing authorities.❜
> *(Romans 13: 1)*

Christians believe it is wrong to commit crimes, and that there are serious consequences for society if crime is allowed to go unpunished. Christians therefore would support the aims of the criminal justice system. Christianity teaches that revenge is not the right response to crime (*Romans 12: 19*).

There are stories and teachings within the Bible which emphasise the importance of love and understanding where crime is involved. Jesus demonstrated a radical response to crime in *John 8: 1–11*. The Jewish leaders brought to him a woman who had been caught in the act of **adultery**, which was against the law at the time, and for which the punishment was being stoned to death. They wanted to trick Jesus: if he agreed with this ruling, he would be sentencing her to death; and if he told them to release her, then he would be breaking the Commandments. However, Jesus said:

> ❛**Let any one of you who is without sin be the first to throw a stone at her.**❜
> *(John 8: 7)*

What forms of cybercrime can you think of? What are **STRETCH** the particular challenges of this kind of crime?

What do you think Jesus means here? **SUPPORT**

The woman was saved, but Jesus warned her to change her behaviour:

> ❝"Woman, where are they? Has no one condemned you?" "No one, sir," she said. "Then neither do I condemn you," Jesus declared. **"Go now and leave your life of sin."** ❞
>
> *(John 8: 10–11)*

USEFUL TERM

Rehabilitate: restore someone back to a law-abiding life

This story emphasises the importance within Christianity of showing mercy, but also of turning away from a life of sin. It can be a challenging story to apply to the modern day, because there are certainly occasions when the law is imposed by those who are not 'without sin'. Otherwise, no one would ever be found guilty of a crime and the legal system would collapse. However, the story does show the importance for Christians of being aware of one's own shortcomings before judging others, even within a rigid legal framework.

D A painting from the sixteenth century, showing Jesus and the woman accused of adultery

How do Christians work to end crime?

Although most Christians agree with the use of imprisonment, many are concerned that prisoners need greater help to change their lives and avoid offending again. Many Christians see it as their duty to help **rehabilitate** criminals to achieve a crime-free life.

Some Christian groups support people when they are released from prison – for example by helping them to find a job and somewhere to live.

CASE STUDY: CHRISTIAN ORGANISATIONS

Prison Fellowship

Prison Fellowship is a Christian organisation that offers prisoners practical support and prayer. Volunteers run Bible study and prayer groups in prisons and aim to put their Christian faith into action by showing justice and mercy. They also run restorative justice programmes to help prisoners understand the impact of their crimes on victims and the community, which is thought to help reduce reoffending (see 2.6).

E A chapel in a Lancashire prison

Street Pastors

Street Pastors is a Christian group that trains volunteers from local churches to patrol the streets at night, offering practical help and prayer to people coming out of pubs and clubs. They look after people who are potentially vulnerable, and they also aim to calm people down who have the potential to cause distress to others, for example if they have consumed too much alcohol. Street Pastors also offer care, listening and help to young people in schools and colleges, and organise prayer for the community.

F Street Pastors offer practical help and prayer to people who are out at night

BUILD YOUR SKILLS

1   Create a mind-map to help you revise this topic. Make sure you include:
    - types of crime, causes of crime, and the problems created by crime
    - Christian teachings and principles about crime
    - two ways that Christians work to end crime.

2   Read *John 8: 1–11*. What does this story teach Christians about the nature of Jesus? How do you think this story would impact on the life of a Christian?

3   Choose either the Prison Fellowship (www.prisonfellowship.org.uk) or Street Pastors (www.streetpastors.org) to research further. What are the aims of these organisations? What principles are these aims founded on?   **STRETCH**

SUMMARY

- A crime is an action that is against the law.
- Christians believe people should obey the law and not commit crime.
- Christianity teaches that revenge is not the correct response to crime, and that love and understanding can turn people away from a life of sin.
- Christian groups and individuals work with criminals and vulnerable people to try to end crime.

EXAM-STYLE QUESTIONS

a   Outline **three** possible causes of crime. (3)

c   Explain **two** Christian teachings about crime. In your answer you must refer to a source of wisdom and authority. (5)

What does Christianity teach about good and evil actions?

Most Christians use the word 'good' to mean acting correctly in accordance with God's will. The Bible teaches that good actions should be done discreetly, not to make yourself look good to others:

> ❝... when you give to the needy, do not let your left hand know what your right hand is doing, so that your giving may be in secret. Then your Father, who sees what is done in secret, will reward you. ❞
> *(Matthew 6: 3–4)*

Most Christians see 'evil' actions as those that go against God by being immoral, and cruel to others – the worst kind of 'bad'. Christians believe that God will judge people by their actions, and reward or punish them accordingly:

> ❝... those who have done what is good will rise to live, and those who have done what is evil will rise to be condemned. ❞
> *(John 5: 29)*

What is the nature of evil actions?

For Christians, evil is an abuse of the **free will** which they believe God gave them so that they could choose right from wrong. Some Christians believe in the existence of the devil (Satan), and that he persuades people to perform evil actions, as in the temptation of Eve in the Garden of Eden. Others, who do not believe in the devil, claim that people do evil things because of influences and experiences in their lives which distract them from God's will.

However, there is a debate regarding responsibility and evil actions:

- If someone commits an evil action because the devil tempted them to do so, can they be held responsible for it?
- If a person carries out an evil action because of circumstances in their life beyond their control, can they be held responsible for it?

How do non-religious people view suffering?

Non-religious attitudes can vary, and may include the following:

- Suffering is inevitable and meaningless.
- Suffering can be caused by people's greed and foolishness.
- Often, those who suffer most are not to blame.
- Humans should work to remove the causes of suffering.
- People should try not to cause harm to others.

SPECIFICATION FOCUS

Christian teachings about good, evil and suffering: Christian teachings about the nature of good actions and how they are rewarded and the nature of evil actions; non-religious attitudes (including atheist and Humanist) about why people suffer, including believing in religion, and Christian responses to them; divergent Christian teachings about why people suffer, including the Parable of the Sheep and Goats (Matthew 25: 31–46).

USEFUL TERM

Free will: having the freedom to choose what to do

Ⓐ The serpent in *Genesis 3*, believed to represent Satan, tempted Eve to sin

CASE STUDY: A HUMANIST PERSPECTIVE

Because we don't believe in any divine or supernatural reality, Humanists are not faced with the 'problem' of how a good, omnipotent, all-knowing God can permit suffering. Given that there is no meaning as such to the universe, I am not troubled with questions about why suffering exists [...] when faced with human suffering, we know there is no supernatural power we can turn to; we are on our own as individuals and as a human community. For many, life is a struggle. We grieve; we fail; we experience feelings of disappointment and desolation. Humanists don't escape this reality. We respond to suffering, whether caused by nature or by human failings, by seeking to relieve the pain, understand the factors that caused suffering, and limit the damage that is being done. Everything we do to alleviate and overcome suffering in the world is worthwhile.
(Alan, Humanist)

Some non-religious people would argue that religion causes suffering:

- It imposes rules on people.
- People feel guilty for not reaching an impossible standard.
- Some religious groups may defend or promote their religion with war and violence.

Christians would respond that:

- Many causes of suffering have nothing to do with religion, and much more to do with human greed and foolishness.
- An important principle in Christianity is grace, meaning that people can freely receive forgiveness for wrong-doings and not live lives of guilt (see 1.5).
- Christianity reduces suffering by encouraging people to treat each other with compassion and love.

Why is Alan not troubled with questions about why suffering exists? SUPPORT

What do Christians believe about why people suffer?

Many Christians believe the following about suffering (see 1.8):

- Suffering is caused by humanity going against the ways of God.
- Suffering is the result of sinful action.
- Suffering can enable people to learn and become better people.
- Suffering is a part of life, and people have a responsibility to care for and comfort those in need.

However, when asked the question, 'Why do people suffer?', Christians would often say that there is no easy answer. Many Christians themselves experience suffering and they would likely experience the same confusion and difficulty in understanding why this happens as other people would. When others suffer, Christians would try to model God's love by coming alongside those who are hurting, trying to help, and empathising with the situation, rather than being quick to offer unsatisfactory answers.

An important Christian teaching which supports this approach is a parable taught by Jesus in Matthew's Gospel, called the Parable of the Sheep and the Goats. Rather than explaining why people are hungry or homeless, the parable shows God's required response of Christians helping to relieve the suffering of others. The parable suggests those who do this will be rewarded by God, and those who do not will be punished. Jesus taught that when people help others, it is as if they are helping him:

> 'For I was hungry and you gave me something to eat, I was thirsty and you gave me something to drink, I was a stranger and you invited me in, I needed clothes and you clothed me, I was sick and you looked after me, I was in prison and you came to visit me [...] **whatever you did for one of the least of these brothers and sisters of mine, you did for me.** '
> (Matthew 25: 35–36, 40)

> 'Truly I tell you, whatever you did not do for one of the least of these, you did not do for me [...] **they will go away to eternal punishment, but the righteous to eternal life.** '
> (Matthew 25: 45–46)

Read and make notes on the whole parable in *Matthew 25: 31–46*. **STRETCH**

 B The Parable of the Sheep and the Goats shown in stained glass windows in a church in Norfolk

SUMMARY

- Christians believe that 'good' actions are in accordance with God's will and 'evil' actions go against God; God will judge people by their actions.

- Some non-religious people believe religion can cause suffering.

- The Parable of the Sheep and the Goats teaches that Christians should model God's love by helping those who are suffering.

BUILD YOUR SKILLS

1. With a partner, write down three actions that you consider to be 'good', and three actions that you consider to be 'evil'. Can you say why you chose those examples? **SUPPORT**

2. How does a Christian decide which actions are good and which are evil? Write a short paragraph to explain how, and include a Christian teaching.

3. Using the information in this topic, copy and complete the following table:

Does religion cause suffering?		
Non-religious arguments	Christian responses	Which argument is strongest and why?

EXAM-STYLE QUESTIONS

b Explain **two** non-religious arguments as to why people suffer. (4)

d 'Religion only makes suffering worse.'
Evaluate this statement considering arguments for and against. In your argument you should:
- refer to Christian teachings
- refer to non-religious points of view
- reach a justified conclusion. (12)

2.4 Punishment

SPECIFICATION FOCUS

Christian attitudes towards punishment: the nature of punishment; divergent Christian attitudes towards the use of punishment, the nature and meaning of biblical teachings about punishment, including Luke 12: 35–48; Christian teachings on why punishment can be regarded as justice and why punishment might be needed in society.

What is the nature of punishment?

In our society there are laws which all citizens must obey; otherwise they face punishment. Judges decide on an appropriate punishment for a convicted offender. The more serious the crime is, the harsher the punishment will be. Several different types of punishment are used in the UK. The most common are:

- **Imprisonment:** This is for the most serious offences. Sentences can vary from a few weeks to a life sentence.
- **Community Orders:** These are for less serious offences. The court orders an offender to work in the community for between 40 and 300 hours.
- **Curfew Orders:** These are limited restrictions on liberty; for example, a person must be in their home from 7:00pm to 7:00am every day for six months.
- **Fines:** These are mainly for traffic offences such as speeding.

Divergent Christian attitudes towards the use of punishment

There are different views among Christians about how and why criminals are punished. On one end of the spectrum is the idea that punishments should inflict pain of some sort on the criminal, and that the amount and type of pain should be determined by the seriousness of the crime committed. This theory of punishment is called 'retribution' (see 2.5).

Some Christians would support such a view because they would emphasise the importance of justice, and they may therefore argue in favour of more extreme punishments such as the death penalty (see 2.8) if they believe the crime is serious enough. They would also argue that if criminals are not punished appropriately then we are ignoring the pain of the victims of crime who have suffered unfairly at the hands of criminals.

On the other side is a view of punishment which is sometimes called 'humanitarian'. This views 'retributive' punishments as acts of revenge, which are therefore wrong. 'Humanitarians' would argue that the only reason for punishing a criminal is to help the criminal to change their ways and become a better person. Therefore, you must never do anything to harm the criminal.

For humanitarians, the only sorts of punishment that would be acceptable would be those that help the criminal to face up to what he or she has done, like prison or community sentences. Many Christians think this is more in line with Jesus' teaching on mercy.

> **STRETCH**
> C S Lewis (a twentieth century Christian writer) argues that only a 'retributive' theory of punishment respects the rights of human beings – including the rights of the criminal who has a right to be punished only to the extent that he or she deserves. What do you think?

> **STRETCH**
> The Church of England bishops stated in 1999 that they 'recognise the need to reintegrate offenders into the community through prison and community based programmes and in partnership with employment and accommodation schemes'. Why is this a humanitarian view?

Biblical teachings about punishment

The Bible highlights the importance of justice and the need for punishment, but it must always be fair. Jesus said:

> ❝Anyone who sets aside one of the least of these commands and teaches others accordingly will be called least in the kingdom of heaven.❞
> *(Matthew 5: 19)*

> ❝You have heard it was said, "Eye for eye, and tooth for tooth". But I tell you, do not resist an evil person. If anyone slaps you on the right cheek, turn to them the other cheek also.❞
> *(Matthew 5: 38–39)*

> ❝**Do not judge, or you too will be judged** [...] first take the plank out of your own eye, and then you will see clearly to remove the speck from your brother's eye.❞
> *(Matthew 7: 1, 5)*

A Speed cameras catch motorists who are speeding; the punishment is usually a fine

These teachings say the following:

- People who disobey the law of God, and encourage others to do the same, will receive punishment.
- Revenge is not the right course of action, and violence should not be escalated; it should be met with peace.
- A person should reflect very carefully on their own behaviour before pointing out the sins of another person. Those who are hypocritical will be judged.

In Luke's Gospel, Jesus gives a particular example about a master, and his two servants. This teaching explains the consequences for both servants if they disobey the master:

> ❝It will be good for those servants whose master finds them watching when he comes [...] the servant who knows the master's will and does not get ready or does not do what the master wants will be beaten with many blows. But the one who does not know and does things deserving punishment will be beaten with few blows [...] **from everyone who has been given much, much will be demanded.**❞
> *(Luke 12: 37–48)*

B Carrying out community service can improve communities and can give offenders an opportunity to 'pay the price' for their crimes

A modern example would be two students who break **SUPPORT** a school rule, but only one of them knew about the rule. Would you expect them both to be punished? If so, how?

According to Jesus, any servant who does something worthy of punishment will be punished. However, the servant who knew his master's will and still disobeyed him will be punished more severely. This teaching suggests that:

- People will be punished for doing wrong.
- People who have been 'given much', in this case knowledge of the will of the master, will have more expected of them.
- God is just – he knows each individual's circumstances, and will take it all into account when he judges them.

Punishment as justice

Christians believe in justice (see 2.1), and that people should be treated fairly according to the law. If God is just, then he will reward people who deserve reward, and punish people who deserve punishment. As in the story of the master and his servants, Christians believe that God judges based on his intimate knowledge of people's hearts.

Punishment in society

Christians believe that if a society has just laws:

- there must be just and fair punishments to support these laws

- if someone is found to be guilty of an offence after a fair trial, they must be given a just and fair punishment

- punishment can therefore support society.

If laws are seen as unjust or unfair, then people may:

- resent them, and protest against them

- refuse to obey them – for example, campaigns against the so-called Poll Tax and Bedroom Tax

- fight among themselves, possibly leading to a civil war.

 People protesting against the 'Bedroom Tax' – a law that changed the amount of Housing Benefit Entitlement that some people could receive

---

BUILD YOUR SKILLS

1 Why are some people in society punished? Include the words law, crime, and justice in your answer. **SUPPORT**

2 What does the Bible say about punishment? Write three bullet points to summarise three teachings, and include a Bible reference with each one.

3 Can you describe two different Christian attitudes towards punishment? Try to refer to Christian teachings in your response.

4 Read and make notes on *Luke 12: 35–48*. Is punishment as described in this scenario fair and just? Identify any arguments for and against, and then explain your conclusion. **STRETCH**

SUMMARY

- People are punished if they are found guilty of breaking laws; more serious crimes are met with stronger punishments.

- The Bible teaches that punishment should be just and fair.

- Punishment is an important part of justice in a society with just and fair laws.

EXAM-STYLE QUESTIONS

a Outline **three** Christian teachings about punishment. (3)

c Explain **two** different Christian beliefs about punishment. In your answer you must refer to a source of wisdom and authority. (5)

What are the aims of punishment, and how do Christians respond?

There are four different aims of punishment:

1. **Protection**: protecting society from criminals and their actions so that people are safe. This aim suggests that criminals should only be punished if this is necessary to protect society, and the method usually removes the criminal from society. For example, if a criminal is in prison, or (in some societies) has been executed, they are unable to negatively impact society any longer. The Catholic Church supports this aim of punishment.

2. **Retribution**: making criminals pay for their actions according to the seriousness of their crimes. Some Christians support this theory of punishment because they argue it is a just way of treating the criminal and God requires Christians to act justly. C S Lewis, a Christian writer, supported this aim of punishment (see 2.4).

3. **Deterrence**: putting other people off from committing a similar crime. Some people argue that the reason for punishing criminals is to discourage them from committing the crime again and to discourage others from doing it. This aim of punishment is not supported by most Christians. This is because a person is punished in order to stop other people from committing the crime, rather than thinking about what is in the best interests of the prisoner.

4. **Reformation**: helping offenders to understand what they have done wrong and to choose not to do it again. This is a popular view among Christians because it appears to mirror how Jesus treated sinners: he did not condemn them but always encouraged them to change their ways.

What does the Bible teach about punishment?

In the Old Testament, punishment was severe and people could be put to death for murder, adultery, and a range of religious crimes, such as **blasphemy**. A well-known phrase from the Bible is 'eye for eye, tooth for tooth' (*Exodus 21: 24*), meaning that a criminal should suffer as much as their victims have. Some Christians use this bit of scripture to support the death penalty (see 2.8), but others argue that this passage was meant to limit the amount of revenge a person could take in a world where vengeance often went to extremes. Jesus also updates this passage in Matthew's Gospel (see page 60) and instead says that people should never take revenge at all, but always forgive those who have caused harm.

> ❝Peter came to Jesus and asked, "Lord, how many times shall I forgive my brother or sister who sins against me? Up to seven times?" Jesus answered, "I tell you, not seven times, but seventy-seven times".❞
> *(Matthew 18: 21–22)*

SPECIFICATION FOCUS

Christian attitudes towards the aims of punishment: Christian attitudes towards each of the aims of punishment (protection, retribution, deterrence and reformation); the nature and meaning of biblical examples of teaching about punishment, including Galatians 6: 1–10.

STRETCH

In the Catechism of the Catholic Church it states 'the traditional teaching of the Church does not exclude recourse to the death penalty, if this is the only possible way of effectively defending human lives against the unjust aggressor' (*CCC, 2267*). What does this mean? What aim of punishment does this support?

A Dangerous criminals can sometimes be put into close supervision centres (known as 'solitary confinement') . What do you think is the main aim of this punishment?

In this teaching in *Matthew 18: 21–22*, Jesus goes even further to make it clear that there are no limits on how much or how often a person should forgive. When Peter asks his question, he thinks 'seven' is a lot of times and he thinks Jesus will congratulate him on being so generous. But Jesus makes it clear that even 'seven' times is not enough and when he says seventy-seven times he is making it clear that forgiveness should never stop. 'Seventy-seven times' means 'an infinite number of times.'

In *Galatians*, Paul makes it clear that Christians should always deal gently with sinners:

> ❝ **If someone is caught in a sin, you who live by the Spirit should restore that person gently.** But watch yourselves, or you also may be tempted. Carry each other's burdens and in this way you will fulfil the law of Christ. ❞
> *(Galatians 6: 1–2)*

According to this teaching, Christians should help sinners to come back to a right way of living, because they too can be tempted to sin, and they would be glad to be treated gently when they do.

Elizabeth Fry, the eighteenth-century prison reformer, said, 'Punishment is not for revenge, but to lessen crime and reform the criminal.' In many ways she sums up the mainstream Christian attitude to punishment. When in *John 8* Jesus forgives the woman caught in the act of adultery, he also adds, 'Go and leave your life of sin.' Teachings like this show that the ultimate goal of punishment is always to rehabilitate. The Bible also teaches the need to protect the weak and vulnerable (*Psalm 82: 3*) and Christians therefore accept that it is sometimes necessary to restrict a person's freedom for the protection of the wider society.

B Rehabilitation schemes can involve prisoners being trained in new work skills

BUILD YOUR SKILLS

1. The four aims of punishment can be difficult words to remember. In pairs, come up with ways to remember them, and test each other on their spellings and definitions. **SUPPORT**

2. Why do Christians have different views about the aims of punishment? Refer to Christian teachings in your answer.

3. Read *Matthew 18: 21–22* again. Is Jesus right to say that forgiveness should never stop? Why would someone disagree with him? Explain your answer. **STRETCH**

SUMMARY

- There are several aims of punishment: protection; retribution; deterrence; reformation, and the severity of punishment is proportionate to the severity of the crime.

- The New Testament teaches that while offenders should be punished, they should also be forgiven and given a second chance.

- Many punishments include opportunities to rehabilitate criminals and Christians would therefore agree that these punishments are correct.

USEFUL TERMS

Blasphemy: disrespect towards God or something considered sacred

Deterrence: discouragement from doing something, for example carrying out a criminal act

Protection: keeping someone or something safe from harm, for example criminal activity

Reformation: changing something (or someone) for the better

Retribution: punishment given in revenge for a wrong that has been done

EXAM-STYLE QUESTIONS

b Explain **two** Christian views on the different aims of punishment. (4)

d 'Reformation is more important than retribution.' Evaluate this statement considering arguments for and against. In your argument you should:
- refer to Christian teachings
- reach a justified conclusion. (12)

2.6 Forgiveness

What does Christianity teach about forgiveness?

Forgiveness means that the victim of a criminal act decides not to feel resentful and angry towards the person who harmed them. It does not mean forgetting or ignoring what happened, or letting the offender go free. Forgiveness, through words or actions, can allow both the victim and the offender to move on. Forgiveness can be a very hard thing to do, and many victims never do it.

A core Christian belief is that Jesus died in order that everyone can receive God's forgiveness for their wrongdoing, if they truly repent (see 1.5). God's nature is forgiving, and therefore Christians believe they should be too. The Bible teaches that people should forgive their enemies and those who hurt them, as shown in 'The Lord's Prayer' (*Matthew 6: 12*).

How and why are offenders forgiven by the community?

Justice means that people should be treated fairly. Where possible, offenders are given the opportunity of rehabilitation to help them to reform and to lead a law-abiding life. This is not only for their own benefit; it is also in a community's best interests for the person not to **reoffend**.

For people who have been imprisoned, rehabilitation may work like this:

> Offender commits crime and is convicted

⬇

> Offender is rehabilitated through an **Offender Behaviour Programme**; rehabilitation may include learning a new trade or studying to pass exams

⬇

> Offender is released and is helped to find work and accommodation, and make a new start. (People convicted for the most serious offences might never be released.)

Some feel that it is unfair that society pays for rehabilitation services that benefit people who have committed crimes against society. However, others think it is important for society to forgive ex-offenders, so that they can learn to participate positively in the community. Without support, ex-offenders might have difficulty integrating into the community, and might resume criminal activities.

SPECIFICATION FOCUS

Christian teachings about forgiveness: Christian teachings and responses to the nature of forgiveness and biblical teachings about it; how offenders are forgiven by the community and why this is needed; Christian teachings about the nature of restorative justice, examples of its use by Christian organisations and why it is important for criminals, including Matthew 5: 21–26.

USEFUL TERMS

Offender Behaviour Programme (OBP): scheme intended to reduce reoffending by tackling issues associated with crime

Reconcile: restore friendly, peaceful or agreeable relations with someone

Reoffend: return to criminal behaviour

Restorative justice: a form of rehabilitation in which criminals are given the opportunity to meet victims of crime

A Working in prison, for example in a laundry, can be part of a prisoner's rehabilitation

What is restorative justice?

Restorative justice gives criminals the opportunity to meet victims of crime. The criminals learn about the impact crime has had on victims' lives. Those in favour of restorative justice say that it rehabilitates criminals quickly, and it can enable them to be released from prison earlier, or not to have to go to prison at all, which reduces pressure on overcrowded prisons. In addition, it takes the suffering of the victims seriously and encourages the criminal to face up to the harm they have caused.

Many Christian organisations are involved in trying to reform the justice system and use restorative justice to help both victims and those who have committed crimes. For example, the Christian charity Prison Fellowship has a programme called Sycamore Tree which teaches prisoners about the principle of restorative justice.

Read *Luke 19: 1–10*. How does Sycamore Tree link to this passage? Do you think this is a good name for a Christian charity that focuses on restorative justice? **STRETCH**

Find out more about Sycamore Tree. What does the programme involve? **SUPPORT**

Why is restorative justice important?

Restorative justice is important for criminals because it helps them to take responsibility for their actions and repair the harm they have caused. It is more likely to lead to the criminal feeling sorry, which will make them far less likely to commit crime in the future. The restorative justice approach also recognises that many people became criminals because of struggles, such as alcohol and drug addiction, which they can be helped to overcome.

In the Sermon on the Mount, Jesus taught that it is very important to forgive and be **reconciled** with people who offend. He urged people not to go to court without first trying to sort things out together:

> ❛Anyone who is angry with a brother or sister will be subject to judgement [...] therefore, if you are offering your gift at the altar and there remember that your brother or sister has something against you, leave your gift there in front of the altar. **First go and be reconciled to them**, then come and offer your gift.❜
> *(Matthew 5: 22–24)*

B Rehabilitation services can include counselling

BUILD YOUR SKILLS

1   In what ways can a community 'forgive' a criminal? Make a list.

2   What is restorative justice and why do Christians support it? Write a short paragraph explaining, and include a Christian teaching.

3   Some people criticise restorative justice as an easy option for those who have committed crimes. What do you think? Explain your views. How would a Christian respond and why? **STRETCH**

SUMMARY

- Forgiveness is a core principle within Christianity.
- Rehabilitation can involve communities forgiving ex-offenders.
- Christians support restorative justice, which gives criminals the opportunity to learn how their crimes affect victims.

EXAM-STYLE QUESTIONS

a   Outline **three** features of restorative justice. (3)

d   'Murderers should never be forgiven.'
    Evaluate this statement considering arguments for and against. In your argument you should:
    - refer to Christian teachings
    - reach a justified conclusion. (12)

What does the Bible say about the treatment of criminals?

The Bible teaches that laws are needed for society to run smoothly and peacefully, and punishing people who break these laws is part of justice. After the Israelites escape from slavery in Egypt, the first thing God does is issue the Ten Commandments (*Exodus 20*) as a way of showing them that if they all want to live freely they have to obey the law.

On the other hand, in the New Testament, Jesus shows the importance of treating prisoners kindly when he says visiting prisoners is one of the actions the righteous will be rewarded for in heaven (see *Matthew 25: 31–46*). For this reason, visiting those in prison is one of the Catholic Church's seven 'corporal works of mercy' – that is, one of the ways they can look after the physical wellbeing of others ('corporal' means 'bodily').

Because Jesus did not condemn the adulterous woman (*John 8*), and instead encouraged her to change her ways, Christians believe that it is important for criminal justice to be 'reformative' – that is, it should help the criminal to reform. They also believe that justice should include mercy, based on the teaching:

> ❝Blessed are the merciful, for they will be shown mercy.❞
> (*Matthew 5: 7*)

Many Christians do not believe that punishment should be used as retribution. Instead, they believe that criminals should:

- serve a fair punishment
- have a second chance to turn their lives around
- receive practical help to reform
- be treated with love.

The Bible also teaches that Christians should speak up for the destitute (destitute means 'lacking'):

> ❝Speak up for those who cannot speak for themselves, for the rights of all who are destitute. **Speak up and judge fairly**; defend the rights of the poor and needy.❞
> (*Proverbs 31: 8–9*)

This teaches that all people should be judged fairly, including people accused of criminal acts. This reflects the justice system today, where the criminal or accused person is innocent until proved guilty, and must be treated fairly.

SPECIFICATION FOCUS

Christian teachings about the treatment of criminals: biblical teachings about the treatment of criminals, including Proverbs 31: 8–9; divergent Christian attitudes towards the use of torture, human rights, fair trial, trial by jury, including the application of ethical theories, such as situation ethics, which may accept the use of torture if it is for the greater good.

HM PRISON
COLDINGLEY

Her Majesty's Prison Service serves the public by keeping in custody those committed by the courts.

Our duty is to look after them with humanity and to help them lead law abiding and useful lives in custody and after release.

HM PRISON SERVICE

RACE RELATIONS POLICY STATEMENT

The Prison Service is committed to racial equality. Improper discrimination on the basis of colour, race, nationality, ethnic or national origins, or religion is unacceptable, as is any racially abusive or insulting language or behaviour on the part of any member of staff, prisoner or visitor, and neither will be tolerated.

 A These signs outside HM Prison Coldingley state how prisoners inside are to be treated

Can you think of any quotes from the Bible that **STRETCH** reflect the statement on the prison wall?

This teaching also emphasises the need for Christians to speak up for *all* who are destitute, which can include victims of crime as well as those who are responsible for it.

What are Christian attitudes towards torture, human rights, and fair trials?

Torture and human rights

Christians believe in **human rights**. Human rights include things like the right to marry and have a family life, the right to privacy, and the right to a fair trial. However, human rights are not just abstract ideals – they are defined and protected by law. In the UK, human rights are protected by the Human Rights Act (1998), which sets out the full list of the fundamental rights and freedoms that everyone in the UK is entitled to.

> ❛The Human Rights Act is an invisible safety net for all of us, and a crucial protection for the most vulnerable: from women fleeing domestic violence to older people in care homes. ❜
> *(Amnesty International)*

Article 2 of the Human Rights Act details the right to freedom from **torture** and inhuman or degrading treatment. Torture occurs when someone deliberately causes serious physical or mental suffering to another person. Torture is not in keeping with any Christian teachings, and most Christians would agree that torture is wrong and should be opposed in every situation.

However, in extreme situations, some Christians may apply different views. For example, imagine someone knew the whereabouts of a bomb, but was refusing to disclose the location. Would it be appropriate to torture this person, in order to find the location of the bomb, if this resulted in many lives being saved? Most Christians would say that torture is always wrong, but it is possible that not all Christians would hold that position in this example.

USEFUL TERMS

Human rights: rights which all human beings are entitled to

Torture: inflicting severe pain on someone

B Nelson Mandela, the late South African President, was a Christian who famously advocated for the humane treatment of prisoners

C The vast majority of Christians oppose the use of torture for any reason

A fair trial

Although the Bible teaches, 'Do not judge, or you too will be judged' (*Matthew 7: 1*), Christians recognise that society needs a justice system. It is important to Christians that the accused person should have access to a **fair trial**. They would support **trial by jury**, which ensures that cases involving criminals are given a proper hearing and that the evidence is carefully considered before a fair judgment is passed.

Situation ethics

Situation ethics is a theory which states that people should do whatever is the most loving thing to do in any given situation. When deciding how to treat a criminal, a person taking a situation ethics approach would look for the most loving thing to do. This is not just in relation to the criminal, but also in relation to those impacted by the criminal's behaviour.

Using situation ethics a person might decide that the most loving thing to do would be to ensure the offender is treated well in prison, to help and educate them, and to let them make a new start in society.

However, situation ethics does not follow any other rules, and therefore a situation ethicist might decide that torture is appropriate if it achieves an outcome that is most loving for the community. Whilst Christians believe it is important to be loving to all people, most Christians would not adopt this approach because they believe the law, the Bible, and other Church teachings forbid torture under any circumstances.

D Hoods like these have been used on prisoners in the UK in the past

🔑 **USEFUL TERMS**

Fair trial: a public hearing by an independent tribunal established by law, that takes place within a reasonable time

Situation ethics: ethical decisions are made according to the specific context of the decision

Trial by jury: a trial where the jury's decision directs the actions of the judge

 BUILD YOUR SKILLS

1 a Make a list of Christian beliefs about how criminals should be treated.
   b Which teachings make the strongest case, in your opinion? Explain your reasons.

2 Consider the approach of situation ethics in this topic, and try to answer the following questions. **STRETCH**
   a How do you know what the most 'loving thing' is?
   b Can torturing a person ever be justifiable? Refer to different viewpoints in your answer.

 SUMMARY

- The Bible teaches that criminals should be treated fairly, but that vulnerable people should be protected from criminals.
- Christians believe that people should be protected by human rights.
- Christians oppose torture; in extreme situations some Christians may have different views.
- Situation ethics requires that the treatment of criminals must take into account the most loving thing to do.

❓ **EXAM-STYLE QUESTIONS**

b Explain **two** reasons why Christians believe punishment should be 'reformative'. (4)

d 'Christians are far too soft on criminals and should support tougher punishments.'
   Evaluate this statement considering arguments for and against. In your argument you should:
   - refer to Christian teachings
   - refer to different Christian points of view
   - reach a justified conclusion. (12)

What is capital punishment?

Capital punishment is commonly known as the death penalty; it is the use of **execution** as the ultimate punishment. In some countries, offences that may result in a death sentence include murder, blasphemy, adultery, drug-dealing, **treason**, and war crimes. The death penalty was abolished in the UK in 1965.

Methods of execution in different countries include:

- firing squad
- hanging
- lethal injection
- stoning
- beheading
- gas chamber
- electric chair.

What is the purpose of the death penalty?

Many people believe that people who commit very serious crimes, such as murder, should be executed. Those in favour of the death penalty could argue that:

- The death penalty means that society can get rid of its most dangerous criminals.
- People who have committed atrocious crimes do not deserve to live.
- If criminals have taken a life, they should pay for it with their own lives.
- Execution is cheaper than keeping a criminal in prison for life.
- The death penalty acts as a strong deterrent (see 2.5).

Arguments against the death penalty

- In countries which have the death penalty, the crime rate does not seem to drop. This suggests that the death penalty does not work as a deterrent.
- Many people have been executed who were later found to have been innocent, for example because of improved DNA testing.
- Terrorists who are executed may be seen as heroes, inspiring more terrorism.
- Killing a criminal could be seen to be just as bad as murder.

What does Christianity teach about capital punishment?

There are teachings in the Old Testament that support the death penalty:

> ❛Whoever sheds human blood, by humans shall their blood be shed.❜
> *(Genesis 9: 6)*

> ❛**Anyone who strikes a person with a fatal blow is to be put to death.**❜
> *(Exodus 21: 12)*

SPECIFICATION FOCUS

Christian attitudes towards the death penalty: the nature and purpose of capital punishment; divergent Christian teachings about capital punishment, including interpretations of Genesis 9: 6, Exodus 21: 8–13 and Matthew 5: 38–48; non-religious (including atheist and Humanist) attitudes towards the use of capital punishment, including the application of ethical theories, such as situation ethics, and Christian responses to them.

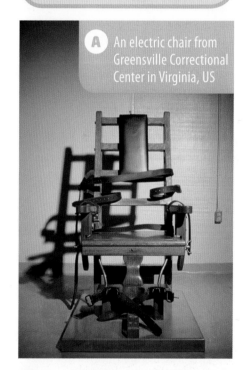

A An electric chair from Greensville Correctional Center in Virginia, US

USEFUL TERMS

Execution: carrying out a sentence of death by killing a person

Treason: being disloyal to one's country by plotting to overthrow the government or ruler

The teachings set out that certain crimes must face the harshest penalty, so murderers, for example, would be killed. Acting in this way not only punished the criminal, but also sent a clear message to society as a whole that these crimes would not be tolerated. This idea of deterrence is the reason why many countries, until relatively recently, made executions a public event.

The difficulty with these teachings is that the aim of punishment, in a Christian context, is to bring about rehabilitation: 'leave your life of sin' (*John 8*). It is also clear that Jesus taught forgiveness and not revenge:

> ❝You have heard that it was said, "Eye for eye, and tooth for tooth." But I tell you, **do not resist an evil person**. If anyone slaps you on the right cheek, **turn to them the other cheek** also [...] love your enemies and pray for those who persecute you.❞
> *(Matthew 5: 38–39, 44)*

These teachings show that there is a tension between how the Old Testament and New Testament deal with the issue of crime and capital punishment. This has caused division among Christians, and there are some Christians (for example Catholics, see *CCC 2267*) who believe in the death penalty while others firmly oppose it.

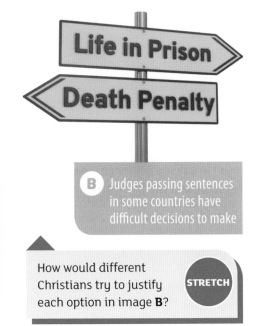

B Judges passing sentences in some countries have difficult decisions to make

How would different Christians try to justify each option in image **B**? **STRETCH**

How do non-religious people view capital punishment?

Non-religious people hold a range of views on capital punishment. Those in favour of it may argue:

- it deters people from committing the most serious crimes
- it gives justice to the victims
- it is a cheaper solution than keeping criminals in prison for life
- it protects society from the worst kind of criminals.

Those against capital punishment may argue:

- capital punishment is barbaric and uncivilised
- waiting in prison to be executed – called waiting on 'death row' – is mental torture
- it is a contradiction to condemn murder but to kill convicts
- most murders are not planned, but are committed in a 'mad moment', so capital punishment has no deterrent effect
- capital punishment does not make victims feel better
- sometimes innocent people are wrongly executed
- all criminals should be given the chance to reform.

C Prisoners on 'death row' sometimes spend years in prison before being executed

> ❝Capital punishment does not seem to deter murder – the US, which is one of the few democracies to retain capital punishment, has one of the highest murder rates in the world [...] Numbers of murders do not rise when capital punishment is abolished.❞
> *(British Humanist Association)*

Can you explain this quote in your own words? Is it for or against capital punishment? **SUPPORT**

CASE STUDY: THE 'OKLAHOMA BOMBER'

On 19 April 1995, a huge home-made car bomb was detonated outside a government building in Oklahoma City, US, killing 168 people (including 19 children) and injuring over 500 others. The bomb destroyed the ten-storey building, which was the headquarters of the Alcohol, Tobacco and Firearms (ATF) agency, and also contained a nursery school. The man responsible was 27-year-old Timothy McVeigh. He said that he had carried out the bombing in revenge for an attack the ATF had made, two years earlier, on a religious group in which 82 people had died. Timothy McVeigh was sentenced to death and was executed by lethal injection on 11 June 2001.

D The explosion ripped the building apart

Amnesty International, the global human rights organisation, says that capital punishment is 'cruel, inhuman and degrading', and it campaigns for an end to capital punishment.

A situation ethicist would consider whether execution is the 'most loving thing' to do in the circumstances.

STRETCH

When might the death penalty be seen as the most loving action to take? For whom would it be loving, and why?

Christian response

Most Christians accept that offenders must be punished and that society must be protected from dangerous criminals. They also believe in the importance of human rights and that offenders should not be treated inhumanely. Most believe that Jesus taught that it is important to love and forgive others, and to offer a second chance – which capital punishment does not do. That is why most Christians do not support the death penalty.

E Many people in the US stage protests against the death penalty

BUILD YOUR SKILLS

1 a Make a list of arguments for and against the death penalty.
   b Which are the strongest arguments and why?

2 How should a Christian respond to the actions of someone like Timothy McVeigh, and why?

3 Are there any circumstances when mass-murderers should be executed? Explain your views.

SUMMARY

- Capital punishment, or the death penalty, is legal in some countries; it is used in the punishment of the most serious crimes.

- There are teachings in the Old Testament that support the death penalty.

- The New Testament teaches forgiveness, rather than revenge.

- Both Christians and non-religious people have a range of views about capital punishment.

? EXAM-STYLE QUESTIONS

a Outline **three** reasons why Christians may support capital punishment. (3)

d 'Execution should be banned in every country.'
   Evaluate this statement considering arguments for and against. In your argument you should:
   - refer to Christian teachings
   - refer to non-religious points of view
   - reach a justified conclusion. (12)

Revision

BUILD YOUR SKILLS

Look at the list of 'I can' statements below and think carefully about how confident you are. Use the following code to rate each of the statements. Be honest!

Green – very confident. What is your evidence for this?

Orange – quite confident. What is your target? Be specific.

Red – not confident. What is your target? Be specific.

A self-assessment revision checklist is available on *Kerboodle*

I can...

- Describe what justice is and say why it is important
- Explain reasons why justice is important for Christians
- Give reasons why justice is important for non-religious people
- Describe what crime is and the problems it can cause
- Give reasons for some of the causes of crime
- Explain Christian views about crime
- Give some examples of how Christians work to end crime
- Give some examples of what Christians believe to be 'good' and 'evil' actions
- Explain how non-religious people view suffering, and how Christians might respond to this
- Describe what the Parable of the Sheep and the Goats teaches about suffering
- Describe different types of punishments given to criminals
- Explain how different Christians and non-religious people view punishment
- Give reasons why punishment is viewed as part of a just and fair society

- List the aims of punishment and describe what they mean
- Describe Christian views on the aims of punishment, with reference to Christian teachings
- Explain what Christianity teaches about forgiveness
- Describe how offenders can be forgiven by the community and say why this is important
- Describe how Christians would view restorative justice
- Explain biblical teachings about the treatment of criminals
- Give examples of how Christians think criminals should be treated
- Describe different Christian views on torture and human rights
- Explain what capital punishment is and why it is used
- Describe how Old Testament teachings on the death penalty differ from New Testament teachings
- Explain the different views that non-religious people have about the death penalty, and give the Christian response to these views.

Exam practice

On these exam practice pages you will see example answers for each of the exam question types: **a**, **b**, **c**, and **d**. You can find out more about these on pages 6–10.

• Question 'a'

*Question **a** is AO1 – this tests your knowledge and understanding.*

> (a) Outline **three** causes of crime. (3)

Student response

Poverty, finance and addiction.

Improved student response

People living in poverty may turn to crime if they cannot buy essential items. A poor social environment might impact a person's sense of right and wrong. Those who are addicted to drugs may steal money for drugs.

 Over to you! Give yourself three minutes on the clock and have a go at answering this question. Remember, this question type requires you to provide three facts or short ideas: you don't need to explain them or express any opinions.

 ✓ WHAT WENT WELL

This student has stated two correct causes of crime.

 ! HOW TO IMPROVE

It's not clear how 'poverty' and 'finance' are two different causes. The student should give a third cause. An even better answer would also give a little more detail to make it clear how these ideas are linked to crime.

• Question 'b'

*Question **b** is AO1 – this tests your knowledge and understanding.*

> (a) Explain **two** reasons a Christian might give about why people suffer. (4)

Student response

Christians believe that people suffer because God gave humans free will. Humans have the right to choose how to behave, and some people abuse that right and cause suffering.

Improved student response

Christians believe that people suffer because God gave humans free will. Humans have the right to choose how to behave, and some people abuse that right and cause suffering.

Another reason a Christian might give is that people sin and turn away from the will of God. God's original plan did not involve suffering, but human sin brought suffering into the world.

 Over to you! Give yourself four minutes on the clock and have a go at answering this question. Try to use two different reasons. Remember, in order to 'explain' something, you need to **develop** your points. See page 9 for a reminder of how to do this.

 ✓ WHAT WENT WELL

This student has given one correct reason and has developed their point with an explanation.

 ! HOW TO IMPROVE

The question asks for **two** reasons. To improve the answer, the student will need to make a second point and develop it. See the 'improved student response' opposite for suggested corrections.

• Question 'c'

*Question **c** is AO1 – this tests your knowledge and understanding.*

> (c) Explain **two** different Christian beliefs about the use of punishment.
> In your answer you must refer to a source of wisdom and authority. (5)

Student response

Many Christians believe that punishments should be tough so that other people won't carry out criminal acts. However, most Christians highlight the need for fair punishments that encourage offenders to change their ways.

Improved student response

Many Christians believe that punishments should be tough so that people will be deterred from carrying out criminal acts. This belief is often coupled with the need for offenders to be punished so as to 'pay the price' for their crimes. Indeed, the Bible says; 'You have heard it said, 'eye for eye, tooth for tooth' (Matthew 5: 38).

However, most Christians highlight the need for fair punishments that encourage offenders to change their ways and come back into society as law-abiding citizens. They would argue that punishment should not be a time of revenge, but of rehabilitation – giving offenders the opportunity to prepare for life outside prison.

 Over to you! Give yourself five minutes on the clock and have a go at answering this question. Remember, you need to write two developed points, one of which needs to be supported by a source of wisdom and authority.

 ✓ WHAT WENT WELL

This student has correctly identified two different Christian beliefs about the use of punishment.

 ! HOW TO IMPROVE

Both points require more detail in order to be fully explained, and the student should use specialist vocabulary where possible. As well as this, the student hasn't given a reference to a source of wisdom and authority. See the 'improved student response' opposite for suggested corrections.

• Question 'd'

*Question **d** is AO2 – this tests your ability to evaluate.*

> (d) 'Christians should oppose the death penalty.' Evaluate this statement considering arguments for and against. In your response you should:
> • refer to Christian teachings
> • refer to non-religious points of view
> • reach a justified conclusion. (12)

Student response

The Bible says that people should not kill one another and therefore Christians should not support the death penalty. They might also say that Jesus taught that people should love their enemies. More importantly, the death penalty gives the offender no chance to reform and change their lives and, some say, it is barbaric.

However, some Christians do support the death penalty. They claim that it deters others from carrying out very serious crimes. It also gives justice to the victims and protects society from dangerous criminals. Also, the Bible teaches that 'Anyone who strikes a person with a fatal blow is to be put to death' (Exodus 21: 12).

There are convincing arguments on both sides and maybe the best conclusion is to say that the death penalty should only be a last resort and only when the offender is definitely guilty.

Improved student response

It could be argued that all Christians should oppose the death penalty. This is because the Bible says that people should not kill one another – in fact, this is one of the Ten Commandments which all Christians believe they should obey. Jesus also taught that people should love their enemies, which means that they should show love and mercy when they might otherwise judge or punish someone. More importantly, the death penalty gives the offender no chance to reform, and an important principle in Christianity is rehabilitation – Jesus gives all people a second chance.

Christians who oppose the death penalty might also agree with the non-religious arguments against it. For example, the British Humanist Association argues that capital punishment actually does not deter murder, which is one of its main aims. Also, modern advances in DNA have revealed that many people have been wrongly executed. This side of the argument is especially strong – if the death penalty can be wrongly used, how could anyone support it?

However, some Christians, and non-religious people, do support the death penalty. They claim that it deters others from carrying out very serious crimes. It also gives justice to the victims and protects society from dangerous criminals. Also, for Christians there are passages in the Bible that support their view, for example 'Anyone who strikes a person with a fatal blow is to be put to death' (Exodus 21: 12).

In conclusion, I think the statement is a strong one. There does not seem to be clear evidence that the death penalty deters crime, and in an imperfect world it is possible for wrongly accused people to lose their lives. Christians should also weigh up Old Testament teachings against the life and example of Jesus, which clearly offers all people a second chance. I think all people – not just Christians – should oppose the death penalty.

Over to you! Give yourself twelve minutes on the clock and have a go at answering this question. Remember to refer back to the original statement in your writing when you give different points of view, and make sure you cover each of the bullet points given in the question.

WHAT WENT WELL

The student explains two different Christian viewpoints, referring to relevant sources of wisdom and authority, and they have reached a partially justified conclusion.

HOW TO IMPROVE

The student has not referred to non-religious points of view, which are required by the question. A better answer would link back to the statement in the question regularly, and use it to evaluate each argument before reaching a fully justified conclusion. A better answer would also aim to use specialist vocabulary. Have a look at this improved version of the student response.

BUILD YOUR SKILLS

In your exams, you'll need to make sure you use religious terminology correctly. Do you know the meaning of the following important terms for this topic?

justice   protection

reformation   fair trial

human rights   retribution

restorative justice

deterrence   death penalty

situation ethics

Humanist   atheist

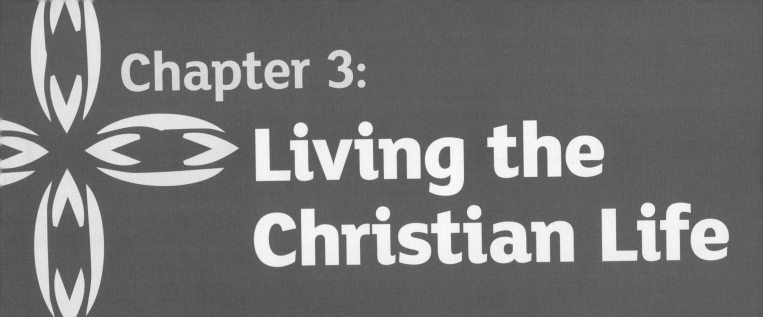

Chapter 3:
Living the Christian Life

3.1 Christian worship

SPECIFICATION FOCUS

Christian worship: liturgical and non-liturgical forms of worship, including activities which are informal and individual, including reference to the *Book of Common Prayer*; when each form might be used and why; divergent Christian attitudes towards the practices, meaning and significance of liturgical and non-liturgical forms of worship in Christian life today, with reference to denominations which worship with less structure such as some Pentecostal churches.

Living the Christian life is a decision on the part of an individual to live as a follower of Jesus. This chapter looks at the various activities that these followers take part in. Although these activities have strong similarities, there are clearly different emphases and divergent attitudes represented among different Christian **denominations**. These differences are often clearest between one denomination and another, but this is not always the case, and it is worth noting that the larger denominations (for instance Anglicans and Catholics) often have a wide range of styles represented within the same denomination.

Worship is when religious believers express their love and respect for, and devotion to, God. It is a time when Christians can thank God, ask his forgiveness, and pray for themselves, other people and the world at large. It helps them to feel closer to God.

Liturgical and non-liturgical worship

Christians can worship in different ways:

- **liturgical** worship: usually following an agreed form of words (often the congregation follow the words in a service book or on an overhead screen).
- **non-liturgical** worship: although the service will have a clear structure, there will be no, or very few, set words other than the words to songs.
- individual worship: quiet worship alone in a person's own home.

The Anglican Church has both liturgical and non-liturgical services. An Anglican service, from the *Book of Common Prayer* or the more recent service book *Common Worship*, contains set services. The text in ordinary type indicates when the priest or service leader should read, and the text in bold type indicates when everyone should read together. Here is an example from an Anglican communion service:

The Lord be with you
All   and also with you.

Lift up your hearts.
All   We lift them to the Lord.

Let us give thanks to the Lord our God.
All   It is right to give thanks and praise.

It is right to praise you, Father, Lord of all creation;
in your love you made us for yourself.

When we turned away
you did not reject us,
but came to meet us in your Son.
All   You embraced us as your children
and welcomed us to sit and eat with you.

A The Anglican communion service is an example of liturgical worship

B Various denominations use modern styles of worship in both liturgical and non-liturgical services

STRETCH

Music is an important feature of liturgical and non-liturgical worship. It is used to praise and express belief in God. Find out what types of music are used in worship and the titles of some specific pieces. Why do you think music like this is so important to worshippers?

Methodists and Catholics have service books like this too. The Anglican denomination also has an informal, non-liturgical service. The structure of that service usually follows a pattern of prayer (see 3.3), sung worship, Bible reading and a **sermon**. There is very little prescription as to what prayers are said or what songs are sung. This style of service might also be found in a Catholic church, but would be more common in Baptist and Pentecostal churches. There would, however, be considerable stylistic differences in the sung worship elements of each of those services. The instruments would also vary from organ music, which traditionally may be more familiar in a Methodist or Baptist setting, to brass bands in a Salvation Army setting, to electric guitars and drums in a Pentecostal setting. By this point in the twenty-first-century, however, all styles of instrument and worship could be found in all denominations.

The Book of Common Prayer

The *Book of Common Prayer* (BCP) is the oldest Anglican service book. It was written in the sixteenth century by Thomas Cranmer, and modified in 1662. Many of its prayers and services are still used today. The BCP also contains: the special services for ordaining priests and bishops; baptism, wedding and funeral services; the **creeds**; the 39 Articles (see 3.2); and special prayers for each week of the year. Here is a prayer from the BCP that has been said since the seventeenth century:

> ' Lighten our darkness, we beseech thee, O Lord;
> and by thy great mercy defend us from
> all perils and dangers of this night;
> for the love of thy only Son, our Saviour, Jesus Christ.
> Amen. '
> *From the Book of Common Prayer*

Divergent Christian attitudes

As we have seen, liturgical and non-liturgical forms of worship occur in various different denominations, and most Christians worship using both forms. However, some Christians prefer one over the other. For example, Christians who value liturgical worship find comfort in using words that may well have been said for

USEFUL TERMS

Creed: a statement of firmly held beliefs; for example, the Apostles' Creed or the Nicene Creed

Denominations: the name given to the main groups within the Church

Liturgical: a set form of worship, usually following agreed words

Non-liturgical: a form of worship which is not set

Sermon: a talk or teaching from a church leader

Worship: believers expressing love and respect for, and devotion to, God

decades, or, in the case of the *Book of Common Prayer*, for centuries. There is also some security in knowing exactly the pattern the service will follow, the length of time it will take, and usually that the form of words used have been authorised by a particular denominational hierarchy.

The non-liturgical service pattern is far more common in charismatic churches, such as Pentecostal churches and an increasing number of Anglican churches, and in these churches the emphasis is placed on 'following the Spirit'; in other words, listening to God and following his lead in worship. Christians who value non-liturgical worship tend to appreciate the fact that they have more freedom to express their worship – this might involve lifting hands or even dancing. Typically the sung worship element may be of any length, the service may or may not have structured prayers, the service leader has far more control of the service and is able to weave in different aspects, for example a video clip or group discussion. Elements of the service can change during the service, extra songs can be added, or an extended prayer time can be introduced.

Individual worship

Believers often worship God on their own. They may want to praise God for who he is, or so that they can feel closer to him, or they may have a particular problem they want to talk to God about. Individual worship can include prayer, meditation, Bible reading, singing, and quiet thinking.

BUILD YOUR SKILLS

1   Copy and complete the following table for the main ideas about Christian worship in this unit. The first type of worship has been given for you.

Type of worship	What does it involve?	Why is it important for Christians?
Liturgical worship		

2   What is the *Book of Common Prayer* and why is it important to some Christians? Write a short paragraph of explanation.

3   Why might some Christians prefer either liturgical or non-liturgical worship? Try to refer to at least one denomination in your answer.

COMPARE AND CONTRAST

In your exam, you could be asked to **compare and contrast** Christian worship with the practices of another religion you are studying. Create a table that explains the similarities and differences among them.

SUMMARY

- Worship is important because it helps believers express love for God.
- It can be liturgical, non-liturgical, or individual.
- There is a great amount of variety in worship both among and within denominations.

EXAM-STYLE QUESTIONS

a   Outline **three** ways a Christian can worship. (3)

b   Describe **two** differences between Christian worship and that of another religion you have studied. (4)

The sacraments

What are sacraments?

The **sacraments** are particularly important and significant Christian ceremonies. Many Christians think of the sacraments as signs of God's love – a special holy action that shows a religious truth. For some Christians, for example Catholics, sacraments are more than just signs – they are 'effective signs', which means that they bring about the thing that they symbolise. For instance, **baptism** is not just a sign of the forgiveness of sins, it actually brings about the forgiveness of sins.

For something to be a sacrament, it has to be officially recognised by the Church as having been established by Jesus. Churches differ on this matter. Therefore, some ceremonies, such as marriage, might be carried out in all churches, but might not be considered to be an official sacrament in all churches.

The sacraments recognised by different groups

Various denominations within the Church have different views on the sacraments. The biggest denominations are the Catholic, Orthodox and Protestant Churches. In turn, Protestants are divided into groups, such as Anglicans (including the Church of England) and Non-Conformists (e.g. Quakers, Methodists, Salvation Army, and Baptists).

The Catholic Council of Trent (1545–1563) agreed that there were seven sacraments (see image **A**). The Orthodox Church also recognises seven sacraments. In contrast, the Church of England met in 1562 to agree the **39 Articles of Religion**, and Article 25 stated that the Church of England would only recognise two sacraments – baptism and the **Eucharist**. In some Protestant churches, for example the Salvation Army and Quakers, no sacraments are officially recognised.

SPECIFICATION FOCUS

The role of the sacraments in Christian life and their practice in two denominations: the role of the sacraments/ordinance as a whole; the nature and importance of the meaning and celebration of baptism and the Eucharist in at least two denominations including reference to the 39 Articles XXV–XXXVI; divergent Christian attitudes towards the use and number of sacraments in Orthodox, Catholic and Protestant traditions.

USEFUL TERMS

39 Articles of Religion: a historical record of beliefs (or 'doctrines') held by the Church of England

Anoint: apply oil to a person's head as a sign of holiness and God's approval

Sacrament: an important Christian ceremony

A The seven sacraments of the Catholic Church

Sacraments of initiation			Sacraments of service		Sacraments of healing	
Baptism	Confirmation	Eucharist (mass or holy communion)	Marriage	Taking holy orders	Reconciliation (confession)	Anointing the sick with oil

The 39 Articles of Religion

In the mid-sixteenth century, the Church of England had recently split from the Catholic Church, and was feeling the influence of various Protestant denominations. Therefore, in 1562, the bishops and archbishops of England came together to discuss matters of belief. Their eventual agreed beliefs would be published under the heading of the 39 Articles. The Articles cover heaven, hell, baptism, creeds, and much more, but the Articles also make some strong statements against various areas of Catholic belief. From that point onwards, priests of the Church of England would need to agree to the 39 Articles before they could be ordained.

Celebrating the sacraments

The sacraments have two important aspects:

- **Physical side:** this can be felt, touched, seen, smelled or tasted, as, for example, the bread and wine in the Eucharist.
- **Spiritual side:** each sacrament brings a spiritual blessing to the person involved.

Each sacrament has its own special ceremony, which includes some or all of the following features: saying prayers, singing hymns, making vows, or promises, listening to Bible readings, listening to a sermon.

Baptism

Baptism is the ceremony in which a person formally becomes a member of the Church. It was commanded by Jesus in *Matthew 28: 19*.

The Catholic, Orthodox and Anglican Churches all celebrate baptism of infants (babies and young children). The Quakers and Salvation Army do not have formal baptism at all. The Baptist Church baptises people it considers old enough to decide for themselves that they want to be baptised.

In an infant baptism, a priest pours water three times on the child's head to show that the Trinity has come into their life and that their sins have been washed away. The child's parents and godparents publicly declare their beliefs, and hold a lighted candle to symbolise that they and the child have passed from the darkness of sin into the light of Jesus. In the Catholic Church, the candle is lit from the Paschal candle as a sign of faith in the resurrection of Jesus. The child is then welcomed as a member of the Church.

Some denominations, for example Baptist and Pentecostal Churches, do not celebrate infant baptism, and instead baptise people when they are adults. This is because they believe baptism is a choice that should be made as an adult. They do celebrate the birth of infants, however, and usually have a 'dedication' service in which the parents and the church community promise to bring up the child according to Christian values.

Confirmation

When a person freely chooses to conclude the process of baptism, as already begun during their baptism as an infant, they are 'confirmed', usually after attending a course of Bible study. Anglicans usually have to be at least

> ❝ There are two Sacraments ordained of Christ our Lord in the Gospel, that is to say, **Baptism, and the Supper of the Lord.** Those five commonly called Sacraments, that is to say, Confirmation, Penance, Orders, Matrimony, and extreme Unction, are not to be counted for Sacraments of the Gospel... ❞
>
> *(From Article XXV of the 39 Articles of Religion)*

USEFUL TERMS

Baptism: the Christian ceremony that welcomes a person into the Christian community

Eucharist: the ceremony commemorating the Last Supper, involving bread and wine; also called Holy Communion or Mass

> ❝ Therefore go and make disciples of all nations, **baptising them** in the name of the Father and of the Son and of the Holy Spirit... ❞
>
> *(Matthew 28: 19)*

What symbolism can you see in this photo? Can you find out its significance? STRETCH

B An infant being baptised into the Catholic Church

12 years old to be confirmed, Catholics have to be at least 8 years old. There is no confirmation service in the Orthodox Church, and instead of confirmation, Orthodox Christians have the sacrament of Chrismation, which immediately follows baptism, and involves being anointed with holy oil called Chrism.

The confirmation service is held by the local bishop. Those being confirmed make the same statements of belief as the parents in an infant baptism. The bishop lays hands on the person's head as a sign that the Holy Spirit has entered into the person's life. (In the Catholic Church, the laying on of hands is what actually brings about the gift of the Spirit). The person is then welcomed as a full member of the Church.

Eucharist

The Eucharist is accepted by most Christians as a re-enactment of the final meal that Jesus shared with his disciples. At that meal, he spoke of bread and wine as being his body and blood.

The Eucharist is called Mass in the Catholic Church, Holy Communion in the Anglican Church and the Lord's Supper by the Methodists. It is not celebrated by the Salvation Army.

In Catholic and Anglican churches today, the priest prays for God's special blessing on bread and wine, which makes them holy. They are then given by the priest to each person taking part in the Eucharist. Only those who are baptised or confirmed may take part. They each take a small piece of bread or a wafer and a sip from a single cup (chalice) of wine. In the Orthodox Church, Christians receive bread soaked in wine.

Not all Christians see the Eucharist in the same way:

- Catholic and Orthodox Christians believe that the bread and wine change to become the actual body and blood of Jesus. In the Catholic Church this change happens when the bread and wine are blessed and is called transubstantiation. In the Orthodox Church, how or when the bread and wine change is believed to be a mystery.
- Other Christians, including Anglicans, believe that the bread and wine are simply symbolic of Jesus' body and blood to help believers remember his death.
- Catholics believe they should receive the bread and wine at least once a week and some receive it every day.
- Protestants may take the bread and wine less often, perhaps once every few weeks. Some do not receive it at all, for example members of the Salvation Army.

Marriage

The sacrament of marriage reflects God's everlasting love. It is the legal union of a man and a woman, who promise before God that they will love, honour, cherish, and respect each other through sickness, health, through good times and bad times, until they are parted by death.

Taking holy orders

In the Catholic and Orthodox Churches, the sacrament of holy orders means becoming a deacon, priest, or bishop.

> ❝And he took bread, gave thanks and broke it, and gave it to them, saying, "This is my body given for you; do this in remembrance of me." In the same way, after the supper he took the cup, saying, "This cup is the new covenant in my blood, which is poured out for you.❞
> *(Luke 22: 19–20)*

SUPPORT

The **covenant** is an agreement between God and humans, which says that because Jesus died to save people from sin, those who believe in him will have everlasting life in heaven with God.

C The Eucharist involves bread and wine

Catholics believe that priests are descended from Jesus' original Apostles 2,000 years ago. As a result, priests receive the grace and power of the Holy Spirit and have the privileged ability to administer all of the sacraments apart from the sacrament of holy orders. Deacons can administer the sacraments of baptism and marriage, and both priests and deacons can preach.

Like Catholic priests, bishops in the Orthodox Church are believed to be the direct successors of the original Apostles. Orthodox bishops are required to remain celibate, but priests may be married before they are ordained.

Reconciliation

The sacrament of reconciliation (also called confession) is when a person asks forgiveness for the wrongs they have done. For reconciliation to be effective, the person must be genuinely sorry, have spent time preparing their confession, and be ready to receive God's blessing and forgiveness. In return, they know they have done what they could to right the wrong.

Catholic and Orthodox Christians confess their sins to a priest, who, as God's representative on earth, will then give them God's forgiveness. This may involve the person having to 'do penance', such as saying a particular prayer a set number of times, or carrying out positive actions to right the wrongs caused by their sins.

Anointing the sick

The sacrament of anointing the sick is based on teaching in the Bible:

D Anointing the sick

> ❛Is anyone among you ill? Let them call the elders of the church to pray over them and anoint them with oil in the name of the Lord.❜
> *(James 5: 14)*

In the anointing ceremony, the sick person confesses their sins and prays with the priest. They pray that God will heal them or, if they are dying, that God will forgive their sins and grant them everlasting life in heaven. The priest lays hands on the person to enable God's love to work within them and some olive oil is gently rubbed onto their forehead.

 EXAM-STYLE QUESTIONS

a Outline **three** Christian sacraments. (3)
b Explain **two** reasons why sacraments are important to Christians. (4)

 BUILD YOUR SKILLS

1 Copy and complete the following table for the main ideas about the sacraments in this unit.

Sacrament	What is involved?	Which Christians recognise it and why?

2 Explain two different approaches to baptism within Christianity.

3 'In the Eucharist, the bread and wine become the body and blood of Jesus.' Would all Christians agree with this statement? Why or why not?

 SUMMARY

- The sacraments are significant Christian ceremonies which have been recognised by the Church.
- The Catholic and Orthodox Churches recognise seven sacraments, the Church of England recognise two (baptism and the Eucharist), and some churches do not officially recognise any.

What is prayer?

Prayer is a way of communicating with God, usually through words, and having a personal relationship with him. Prayer may offer praise or thanks to God or ask him for forgiveness or other specific things, for example good health. Christians can pray in many different ways – using set or informal prayers, in public or in private, every day or on special occasions.

Set prayers

Most prayers in an Anglican or Catholic church service are set and formal. They are usually read or sung from a text, such as the *Book of Common Prayer*, and follow a set pattern very familiar to believers. The most famous formal prayer is the Lord's Prayer (see figure **A**), which Jesus taught to his followers. It is a special prayer because it covers the needs of all believers.

Informal prayer

Some prayer is much more informal. This type of prayer features in evangelical and charismatic churches, where prayers are not often written down. Instead, prayer tends to be much more spontaneous, because believers say that they are led by the Holy Spirit to choose words to express how they feel at the time.

SPECIFICATION FOCUS

The nature and purpose of prayer: the nature of and examples of the different types of prayer; set prayers; informal prayer and the Lord's Prayer including Matthew 6: 5–14; when each type might be used and why; divergent Christian attitudes towards the importance of each type of prayer for Christians today.

USEFUL TERMS

Prayer: a way of communicating with God

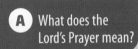

A What does the Lord's Prayer mean?

'Our Father in heaven, —— This is a personal and loving response to God.

hallowed be your name, —— Your name is holy and special.

your kingdom come, —— May God's kingdom come to our world.

your will be done, —— May God's will be carried out.

on earth as it is in heaven. —— May God be in charge.

Give us today our daily bread. —— Give us all we need to survive.

And forgive us our debts, —— Forgive the wrongs we have done.

as we also have forgiven our debtors. —— Help us to forgive those who have wronged us.

And lead us not into temptation, —— Keep us from being tempted to do wrong.

but deliver us from the evil one.' —— Keep us from doing evil.

(Matthew 6: 9–13)

Private prayer

Believers can also pray in private settings, such as their own homes. They might say their prayers aloud or offer them silently to God.

> 'When you pray, go into your room, close the door and pray to your father, who is unseen. Then your Father, who sees what is done in secret, will reward you.'
> *(Matthew 6: 6)*

Special purposes of prayer

Christians use different prayers, depending on what they want to say to God. These can be grouped into different types:

Thanksgiving: to thank God for all that they have.
Contrition: to tell God what they have done wrong and ask for forgiveness.
Supplication: to ask God for something for themselves or others.
Intercession: to ask God to help other people.
Worship: to give honour and respect to God.

Divergent Christian attitudes

Most Christians will use both set and informal prayer to communicate with God. The Lord's Prayer is used regularly in most denominations, as Christians like to follow the example set by Jesus. Christians who prefer to pray using set prayers find comfort in using words that have been said throughout history and that have been authorised by their Church. Reciting these aloud as a community also increases a sense of shared belief and unity. Christians who prefer praying informally might particularly appreciate the personal nature of communicating how they are feeling with God. These Christians also value praying aloud in groups, and those with them will often say 'Amen' after an individual has prayed to show that they agree with the prayer.

B Many Christians feel better by being able to talk directly and privately to God

C *Praying hands*, a drawing by Albrecht Dürer (c. 1508ce)

BUILD YOUR SKILLS

1 Read the Lord's Prayer on page 85. What different things do Christians ask for or say in this prayer? **SUPPORT**

2 Why do Christians pray? Write a short paragraph to explain.

3 If God knows everything, what is the point of praying? What would a Christian argue? **STRETCH**

EXAM-STYLE QUESTIONS

b Explain **two** reasons why prayer is important to Christians. (4)

d 'Prayer should be informal.' Evaluate this statement considering arguments for and against. In your response you should:
- refer to Christian teachings
- refer to different Christian points of view
- reach a justified conclusion. (15)

SUMMARY

- Prayers can be set, informal or private.
- There are prayers for different purposes, and believers differ in their views on the importance of certain types of prayer.

3.4 Pilgrimage

What is pilgrimage?

A **pilgrimage** is a special journey to a place of religious significance. It is undertaken by a pilgrim, who is making the journey in order to increase their religious faith. It may be a long journey to another country or a shorter one to a sacred place nearer to home.

The first Christian pilgrimages date from the fourth century, when travellers visited the Holy Land (now called Israel) to see places linked to the life of Jesus. Early pilgrims also visited Rome, other sites linked to the Apostles and the saints, and places where **visions** of the Virgin Mary were said to have occurred.

Today, pilgrimage is still popular, with Christians making journeys to Rome, the Holy Land, and **shrines** all around the world. A pilgrimage should have a real impact on the pilgrim and involve some or all of the following aspects: feeling closer to God, discovering special rituals, objects and places, having religious and spiritual experiences, praying and meditating, seeking a cure for sickness.

Divergent Christian views on pilgrimage

The Catholic Church teaches about the importance of pilgrimage in the Christian life:

> ❝ Pilgrimages evoke our earthly journey toward heaven and are traditionally very special occasions for renewal in prayer. ❞
> *Catechism of the Catholic Church, 2691*

In other words, pilgrimages are believed to be a special opportunity to pray and experience closeness to God. In many Protestant Churches, pilgrimage is equally important, although the sites of significance may sometimes be different (for example, Christians who do not recognise the authority of the Pope, as Catholics do, may not view a pilgrimage to Rome in the same way).

Some Protestant Churches do not place as much emphasis on pilgrimage. Whilst journeying and praying for the sake of God is something they might encourage, pilgrimage is not considered by them to be a central part of Christian life.

SPECIFICATION FOCUS

Pilgrimage: the nature, history and purpose of pilgrimage, including interpretations of Luke 2: 41–43; the significance of the places people go on pilgrimage; divergent Christian teachings about whether pilgrimage is important for Christians today, with specific reference to Catholic and Protestant understandings; the activities associated with, and significance of, Jerusalem, Iona, Taizé and Walsingham.

SUPPORT

What do you think believers gain from pilgrimage? Is it just a religious holiday?

STRETCH

The Canterbury Tales, written by Geoffrey Chaucer around 1390 CE, is a collection of stories told by pilgrims on a pilgrimage from London to Canterbury Cathedral.

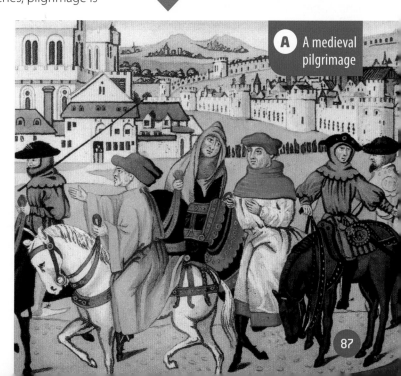

A A medieval pilgrimage

The pilgrimage to Jerusalem

The most famous place of Christian pilgrimage is Jerusalem in Israel (the Holy Land). It is where most of Jesus' ministry took place, so pilgrims feel it is important to go to different sites in the city to think about the events that took place there.

In the Gospel of Luke, Jesus himself made a pilgrimage with his parents to Jerusalem, at the age of 12. When it was time to leave, his parents could not find Jesus. When they finally found him, he was in the temple, sitting and listening to teachers, and he said: 'Why were you searching for me? […] Didn't you know I had to be in my Father's house?' (*Luke 2: 49*). Modern pilgrims aim to follow Jesus' example and look for opportunities to be close to God. Pilgrims today visit:

B Modern pilgrims on the Via Dolorosa, the road believed to have been taken by Jesus on his way to be crucified

- The Mount of Olives, where Jesus often taught his followers
- The Western Wall, remains of the Temple
- The Church of the Holy Sepulchre, where Jesus was crucified and buried
- The room of the Last Supper
- The Garden of Gethsemane, where Jesus was arrested
- The tomb of the Virgin Mary

The pilgrimage to Iona

Iona Abbey, on the island of Iona, off the west coast of Scotland, is one of the UK's oldest sites of pilgrimage. It was founded by St Columba in 563CE and became the focal point for the spread of Christianity throughout Scotland. The abbey was extensively restored in 1899 and in 1938, when the Iona Community was founded. This Christian community is based on worship, peace and social justice, and welcomes all believers to share in this ministry today.

The pilgrimage to Taizé

Another important place for Christian pilgrimage today is a monastic order in the small village of Taizé in central France. The Taizé Community was founded by Roger Schütz, known as Brother Roger, in 1940. Today, it has over 100 members, and thousands of pilgrims visit to share the community's way of life.

The community prays together three times a day and is devoted to peace and justice through prayer and meditation. It seeks to unite people of all races and encourages pilgrims to live in the spirit of kindness, simplicity, and reconciliation. Importance is also placed on music, including songs and chants in many languages.

People who live **monastic** lives, such as **monks** and **nuns**, have chosen to dedicate their lives to prayer and worship, usually whilst living in a **monastery** with others.

SUPPORT

The pilgrimage to Walsingham

A popular English site for Christian pilgrimage is the Shrine of Our Lady of Walsingham in Norfolk.

It is said to be the place where Lady Richeldis de Faverches saw a vision of the Virgin Mary in 1061CE. According to tradition, the Virgin showed Lady Richeldis a vision of the house where the Angel Gabriel told Mary that she would be the mother of Jesus. Lady Richeldis built a copy of the house on the spot where she had the vision. Known as the Holy House, it became a place of pilgrimage.

In the centuries that followed, thousands of pilgrims went to Walsingham, including Henry VIII and Queen Catherine of Aragon. Later in Henry's reign, the shrine was destroyed.

After restoration, Walsingham was re-opened to regular pilgrimage in the 1920s. In 1938 it was enlarged to form the area known today, including a Catholic shrine, an Anglican shrine and the Orthodox Church of St Seraphim. There are often, therefore, pilgrimages of mixed denominations to Walsingham.

BUILD YOUR SKILLS

1   Copy and complete the following table for important pilgrimage sites.

Site of pilgrimage	What does it represent?	Why is it important for Christians?
Jerusalem		
Iona		
Taizé		
Walsingham		

2   a   Which of the following statements, if any, do you agree with? Explain why.
- 'Some sites of pilgrimage are more convincing than others.'
- 'Pilgrims are just wishful thinkers.'
- 'Pilgrimage is still important in today's world.'
- 'On pilgrimage, the journey is as important as the destination.'

   b   With a partner, discuss whether pilgrimages are worthwhile or a waste of time.

3   Many thousands of young people visit Taizé each year (see image **C**). Do you think they have to be Christians to benefit from the visit? Why/why not?

EXAM-STYLE QUESTIONS

a   Outline **three** reasons why pilgrimage is important to Christians. (3)

d   'Every Christian should go on a pilgrimage.'
Evaluate this statement considering arguments for and against. In your response you should:
- refer to Christian teachings
- refer to different Christian points of view
- reach a justified conclusion. (15)

SUMMARY

- Pilgrimage has a very long history and is still important today.
- Jerusalem, Iona, Taizé and Walsingham are important pilgrimage sites.
- Pilgrimage helps believers to understand more about God and their faith.
- It can give believers a strong religious or spiritual experience.

Christians use celebrations to remember and give thanks for the most important events in their faith. Celebrations take different forms to reflect the nature of the event. Some, like Christmas and Easter Sunday, are times of great rejoicing. Others, such as Good Friday, are times for quiet reflection.

Christmas

There are two accounts of the birth of Jesus, given in the Gospels of Luke and Matthew. According to Luke's Gospel, God sent the Angel Gabriel to tell a woman called Mary, who was a virgin, that she would be the mother of God's son. She accepted God's will and became pregnant. She and her husband Joseph travelled to the town of Bethlehem. There, she gave birth to Jesus and was visited by shepherds. The Gospel of Matthew includes an account of the visit of the wise men, or 'Magi', from the east.

The whole season of Christmastide runs for 12 nights after 25 December to 6 January, which is when Jesus was shown to the wise men. The 6 January is therefore called **Epiphany** or Twelfth Night.

As a festival, Christmas shares much in common with other festivals at that time.

- It is just after mid-winter, when the sun begins to shine more and the days start to grow longer.
- It is near the Winter Solstice, when mistletoe was seen as a sign of God's blessing.
- Holly, also a Christian symbol, was used by ancient people as a protection from evil.

In medieval times, Christmas was a time for feasting and fun. However, in the seventeenth century, people were not allowed to have celebrations because they were believed by Puritans to be excessive and a distraction from core Christian beliefs. In 1644 Christmas was banned altogether. Christmas became popular again in the nineteenth century when cards, decorations and Christmas trees were introduced.

Today, Christian churches hold special services, including carol services and a **vigil** before Christmas, midnight mass on Christmas Eve, and a special service of celebration on Christmas morning, which may include a **nativity** play.

A Children's nativity plays are an important part of church life

SPECIFICATION FOCUS

Christian religious celebrations: the nature and history of Christian festivals in the church year, including Christmas and Easter; the significance of celebrating Advent and Christmas; the significance of celebrating Holy Week and Easter, with reference to interpretations of 1 Corinthians 15: 12–34.

USEFUL TERMS

Advent: a season of preparation for Christmas

Epiphany: a moment of suddenly revealing something surprising or great; in the Christian calendar, Epiphany is a celebration of the revelation of Jesus

Holy Week: the week before Easter

Nativity: the birth of someone

Prophecy: a message from God in which he communicates his will

Vigil: staying awake at night in order to pray; also the name given to the celebration of a festival on the eve before the festival itself

B Candlelight vigil

Advent

Advent starts on the Sunday nearest 30 November. It marks the start of the Christian year and is a time of preparation for Christmas. On the first Sunday of Advent, Christians light one of the four candles on Advent wreaths. On each of the next three Sundays before Christmas, they light one more candle. This is to remember the 'light' of Jesus that is about to come into the world.

Holy Week

Holy Week is the week just before Easter, beginning with Palm Sunday and ending with Holy Saturday. It is the final week of Lent, the six-week period of self-examination when most Christians pray, say sorry and try to make amends for their wrongdoings, fast, and give to the poor in preparation for celebrating Jesus' resurrection on Easter Sunday. Holy Week is also a time of solemn church services, as Christians remember the final days and death of Jesus. The following events are remembered during the week:

- **Palm Sunday:** Jesus' arrival in Jerusalem on a donkey, when huge crowds greeted him and threw down palm leaves. This fulfilled an ancient **prophecy** that the Messiah would arrive in this way. Today, Christians receive small palm crosses to remind them of the prophecy and the death of Jesus.

- **Holy Monday:** Mary anointing Jesus with oil at Bethany as a sign of God's approval (*John 12:3*).

- **Holy Tuesday:** Jesus predicting that Judas would betray him and Peter would deny that he knew Jesus.

- **Holy Wednesday:** Judas arranging with the high priests to betray Jesus.

- **Maundy Thursday:** Jesus washing the disciples' feet and the Last Supper. The washing of feet was a symbolic act to show that the disciples must be humble and serve others ('Maundy' means 'commandment'). On this day, churches may hold a meal reflecting the original Last Supper.

- **Good Friday:** Jesus' death on the cross. For Christians, this is a solemn day of processions or re-enacting the events leading up to the crucifixion.

- **Holy Saturday:** Jesus going to hell and preaching to the dead. In the evening, many Christians hold a vigil. For example, on the eve of Holy Saturday, Catholic Christians have an Easter vigil at which they celebrate the resurrection of Jesus. This is the most solemn liturgy that the Catholic Church celebrates.

'Shout, daughter of Jerusalem! See your king comes to you, righteous and having salvation, gentle and riding on a donkey.' (*Zechariah 9: 9*)

'I tell you the truth, one of you is going to betray me.' (*John 13: 20*)

'A new command I give you: Love one another.' (*John 13: 34*)

Easter Sunday

Easter Sunday celebrates the resurrection of Jesus from the dead. Jesus had been buried in a cave tomb with an enormous stone rolled across the entrance. On Sunday morning, Mary Magdalene, then others of Jesus' followers, found that the stone had been rolled away and the tomb was empty. Soon after, they saw Jesus – he had risen from the dead.

In *1 Corinthians 15*, Paul writes to the Corinthian church about the resurrection. Members of the church at the time were in disagreement about whether the dead could be raised. Paul emphasises the fundamental importance of the resurrection to Christianity:

> ‘For what I received I passed on to you as of first importance: that Christ died for our sins according to the Scriptures, that he was buried, that he was raised on the third day... ’
> *(1 Corinthians 15: 3–4)*

He writes, 'by this gospel you are saved' (*1 Corinthians 15: 2*), in other words Christians have access to eternal life because of the resurrection of Jesus.

> ‘And if Christ has not been raised, our preaching is useless and so is your faith. ’
> *(1 Corinthians 15: 14)*

Most Christians today believe in the physical resurrection of Jesus, but some more liberal Christians believe that the resurrection should be interpreted metaphorically. Mainstream and liberal Christians alike celebrate this story on Easter Sunday, worshipping and praising Jesus in church services.

C The empty tomb; which people can you see represented here?

Read the rest of Paul's argument in *1 Corinthians 15: 12–34*. What are his key points? **STRETCH**

BUILD YOUR SKILLS

1   Explain the significance of each of the following: Christmas, Advent, Holy Week, Easter.

2   Which of the following statements, if any, do you agree with? Explain why.
   • 'Easter is about the death of Jesus, not about Easter eggs.'
   • 'The most important Christian celebration day is Easter Sunday.'
   • 'Religious celebrations have no importance in today's world.'

3   According to Paul, why is the resurrection of Jesus so important?

SUMMARY

• Christian celebrations include Advent, Christmas, Holy Week, and Easter.

• These celebrations help believers to remember the importance of events in Jesus' life.

• They also help believers to feel closer to God and understand more about their faith.

? EXAM-STYLE QUESTIONS

a   Outline **three** features of Christmas for Christians. (3)

d   'Easter is the most important Christian festival.'
   Evaluate this statement considering arguments for and against. In your response you should:
   • refer to Christian teachings
   • refer to different Christian points of view
   • reach a justified conclusion. (15)

3.6 The future of the Church

Growth of the Christian Church

Christianity has more followers than any other religion and **Pentecostalism** is one of the fastest growing denominations. There are 2.4 billion Christians in the world today and the number is growing. The biggest increases recently have been in Africa, where there are 541 million Christians, with 33,000 people joining the faith every day. The Church is also growing in Asia and the Middle East, especially in Nepal, China, and Saudi Arabia.

Much of this growth is due to the work of **missionaries**, who preach from the Bible and invite people to **convert** to the Christian faith. However, people in many countries are also actively turning away from traditional beliefs to join faiths that seem to offer more – enthusiasm, lively worship, and a promise of eternal life.

Christianity in the UK

In contrast, the Christian Church in the UK and Western Europe is going through a difficult time. A recent survey noted that although 64 per cent of UK residents say they are Christian, the number of local churchgoers is falling quite rapidly. Many churches closed between 2010 and 2016 – 168 Anglican, 500 Methodist and 100 Catholic.

However, the numbers of people joining Pentecostal and evangelical churches has been steadily increasing. Between 2010 and 2016, 600 Pentecostal churches opened. This growth seems to be driven in part by people coming to live in the UK, particularly from Africa, the Caribbean and South America, but these churches have also seen a steady increase in UK worshippers.

Christian missionary work

The Church has a **mission** to spread the Christian faith. It does this by sending missionaries around the world. As well as preaching to people about Jesus, missionary work may also include working among the poor to build hospitals and schools, nursing, and teaching.

🔍 SPECIFICATION FOCUS

The future of the Christian Church: Church growth, the history and purpose of missionary and evangelical work including reference to Mark 16: 9–20 and John 20: 21–22; divergent ways this is put into practice by Church locally, nationally and globally; Christian attitudes to why evangelical work is important for the Church and for individual Christians.

🔑 USEFUL TERMS

Convert: to change from one set of beliefs to another

Mission: sending individuals or groups to spread the Christian message

Missionary: a person who preaches and invites people to convert to the Christian faith

Pentecostalism: a Protestant movement that puts special emphasis on a direct and personal relationship with God through the Holy Spirit

A A church community in Rwanda, Africa

The history of missionary work

The first missionaries were the original followers of Jesus, who obeyed his command called the Great Commission. With the help of the Holy Spirit, the followers were commanded to preach the gospel to all of creation:

> ❝He said to them, "**Go into all the world and preach the gospel to all creation**. Whoever believes and is baptized will be saved, but whoever does not believe will be condemned."❞
> *(Mark 16: 15)*

> ❝Again Jesus said, "Peace be with you! As the Father has sent me, I am sending you." And with that he breathed on them and said, "**Receive the Holy Spirit...**"❞
> *(John 20: 21–22)*

The most famous early missionary was St Paul, whose mission took him as far as Rome – thousands of miles from where he began. In the following centuries, Christian missionaries went to many other parts of the world.

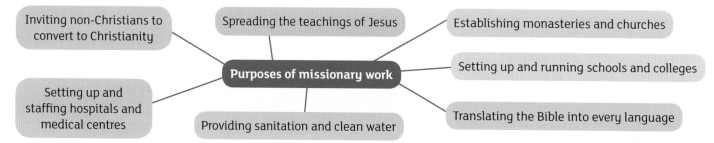

Inviting non-Christians to convert to Christianity

Spreading the teachings of Jesus

Establishing monasteries and churches

Purposes of missionary work

Setting up and running schools and colleges

Setting up and staffing hospitals and medical centres

Providing sanitation and clean water

Translating the Bible into every language

Missionary work today

Many Christians still feel the responsibility to tell others of their faith. Whilst some become missionaries, others show their faith at home in the way they conduct their everyday lives.

Most Christian countries still send missionaries abroad, but they also receive them from elsewhere. Typically, the UK sends out 15,000 missionaries a year, whilst 10,000 others travel into the UK.

However, some people criticise missionary work abroad on the basis that missionaries:

- might only spread Western values
- can infect local populations with foreign germs and diseases
- have caused conflicts and even wars in the past
- could be accused of using natural disasters as an opportunity to 'convert' those who are suffering.

The growth of the Pentecostal Church in Britain is also a type of 'reverse mission', with immigrants drawing people back into churches here.

On a local level, churches are encouraged to be open and welcoming to everyone, not just practising Christians, often holding events to draw non-believers in.

B A school in Cambodia set up by missionaries

Christian evangelistic work

Missionary work involves **evangelism**, preaching the Christian faith in order to invite those of other faiths or none to convert to Christianity. Evangelists are often missionaries, but they might be skilled in preaching to large numbers in their own country.

Evangelists are inspired by biblical teaching to speak clearly, fearlessly and respectfully, and see themselves as following a call from God.

> ❛Pray also for me […] so that I will fearlessly make known the mystery of the gospel…❜
> *(Ephesians 6: 19)*

SUPPORT

The word **evangelism** comes from the Greek word euaggellion, which means gospel or good news.

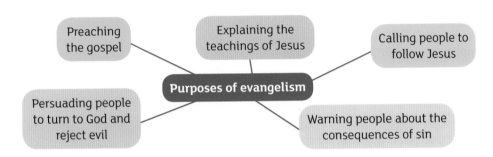

Preaching the gospel

Explaining the teachings of Jesus

Calling people to follow Jesus

Purposes of evangelism

Persuading people to turn to God and reject evil

Warning people about the consequences of sin

USEFUL TERMS

Alpha: a course run by churches and local Christian groups which enables people to find out more about the Christian faith in a relaxed setting

Evangelism: preaching the gospel in order to attract new believers

Evangelism today

Modern evangelists can be very public figures. Some use television, radio, the Internet, social media, drama, music or comedy to communicate their message. A few appear on television's 'God Channel'. Others speak to huge crowds at Christian events.

However, for many Christians today, evangelism is something that happens naturally in conversation and discussion, as they talk about their faith with others.

CASE STUDY: ALPHA

One organised way that churches enable evangelism in a relaxed format is through **Alpha**, which was started in an Anglican church in 1977. At first, it aimed to help church members understand the basics of the Christian faith. It soon began to be used as an introduction for anyone interested in learning about Christianity.

It now offers 'an opportunity to explore the meaning of life' through a series of talks and discussions in all sorts of places from homes to offices, churches to prisons. The idea has now been adopted by other denominations worldwide and has generated related courses such as relationship courses.

C A group of young people taking part in Alpha

Alpha

STRETCH

Find out more about Alpha by visiting **uk.alpha.org**. What happens on a typical course? What questions do people discuss?

The importance of evangelistic work

This work is important for the Church as a whole and for individual Christians. It:

- enables Christians to obey the Great Commission of Jesus
- encourages Christians to tell other people about their faith
- can help the poor and suffering to have hope
- can occur alongside improvements to education and healthcare
- keeps the Christian message alive and relevant to life today
- brings many new Christians to the Church.

BUILD YOUR SKILLS

1   Copy and complete the following table for Christian missionary and evangelical work.

	What does it mean?	Examples	Why is it important for Christians?
Christian mission			
Evangelism			

2   a   Imagine a conversation about evangelism between three teenagers – one is an evangelical Christian, one is a member of another faith, and the third is an atheist. Write a short conversation between them in which:
- each says why their view is right
- each tries to prove that the others are wrong.

b   Which teenager do you think offers the best answers? Why?

3   a   With a partner or in a group, discuss the advantages and disadvantages of:
- evangelising on television
- taking part in the Alpha Course.

b   Write down your conclusions.

SUMMARY

- Christian Church membership is growing globally, but is falling in the UK.
- Missionary and evangelical work preach the Christian faith and invite people to convert to Christianity.
- Missionaries also help the needy.

EXAM-STYLE QUESTIONS

a   Outline **three** purposes of Christian missionary work. (3)

c   Explain **two** reasons why evangelism is important to Christians. In your answer you must refer to a source of wisdom and authority. (5)

3.7 The local church

The importance of the local church to the parish

Most Christians belong to a **parish** – a community of local believers within a particular denomination. The care of the parish and its people is entrusted to a parish priest. The local church building plays an important role in the community's life together. Living in that community encourages individual Christians to put their faith into action in everyday living practices, such as being a good neighbour and caring for those in need.

SPECIFICATION FOCUS

The role and importance of the local church in the local community: how and why it helps the individual believer and the local area; local parish activities, including interpretations of 1 Peter 5: 1–4, ecumenism, outreach work, the centre of Christian identity and worship through living practices.

A place for Christians to gather as a community

A regular pattern of worship through church services

Special services for baptisms, weddings, and funerals

A place to learn about Christian beliefs and way of life

Care and advice from the priest and other church officials

A The parish church is the centre of local religious life

How the local church helps individual believers and the local area

The Bible calls the Church 'the body of Christ' and Christians believe that the Church is holy and belongs to God. The Church's mission is to preach the gospel and to make God's kingdom a reality in their own local community.

Each **local church** follows that mission. It also supports believers in following Jesus' teachings in their own lives, encouraging them to be good people. Local churches carry out their mission in various ways, by:

B Is it really the role of local churches to feed the poor?

- offering the church as a community centre to bring local people together
- giving spiritual support to the sick
- praying for those in need
- supporting groups that campaign for justice and peace
- offering moral guidance
- telling others about Jesus (evangelism)
- **outreach** to children, the poor and the needy
- supporting young adults with advice on jobs, training, finance, and finding a home
- giving friendship and help to the elderly
- raising money for charity.

Should local churches be used just by believers or also by non-believers? **STRETCH**

Ecumenism

There is a movement within the Church that tries to create unity and friendship between different Christian denominations. It is called **ecumenism**. Supporters say that closer union will lead to:

- tolerance of different ideas
- mutual understanding of the Christian faith
- less discrimination and conflict
- friendship among Christians.

 Pope Francis meets Archbishop Justin Welby and his wife Caroline at the Vatican in 2013

BUILD YOUR SKILLS

1 What do these terms mean, and why are they important? Parish, the local church, ecumenism.

2 a What are Christians being taught to do in these Bible verses?

> ❝To the elders among you [...] Be shepherds of God's flock that is under your care, watching over them – not because you must, but because you are willing, as God wants you to be; not pursuing dishonest gain, but eager to serve; not lording it over those entrusted to you, but being examples to the flock. And when the Chief Shepherd appears, you will receive the crown of glory that will never fade away.❞
> *(1 Peter 5: 1–4)*

> ❝Always be prepared to give an answer to everyone who asks you to give the reason for the hope that you have.❞
> *(1 Peter 3: 15)*

> ❝Whoever welcomes one of these little children in my name welcomes me.❞
> *(Mark 9: 37)*

b How might a Christian put each of these teachings into practice today?

USEFUL TERMS

Ecumenism: a movement that tries to bring different Christian denominations closer together

Local church: a meeting place for local believers and the community of believers who gather there

Outreach: an activity to provide services to people in need

Parish: a community of local believers within a particular denomination

SUMMARY

- Parish churches are the centre of local religious life but they also welcome atheists.
- They preach the Christian faith and help the needy.
- They offer advice and special services for the important events in people's lives.
- The different denominations of the Christian Church are working together through ecumenism to create greater understanding with each other.

EXAM-STYLE QUESTIONS

a Outline **three** ways that the local church serves its local community. (3)
b Explain **two** reasons why ecumenism is important to Christians. (4)

What is the role of the Church in the worldwide community?

The Church exists in every nation and aims to have a positive spiritual impact on the world. Its roles include:

- representing Jesus on earth
- bringing the gospel to all people
- helping the poor, the sick, and the needy
- promoting friendships
- bringing together as a community all the people who want to know and love God.

The Church is important within the global community because it encourages peace and harmony between individuals and countries, and teaches and tries to set a good example of living a moral life. It also organises charity work, supports the work of its missionaries and helps Christians in need around the world.

The Church also has powerful influence in debates on:

- abortion
- injustice
- marriage
- moral issues
- political decisions
- poverty
- same-sex relationships.

SPECIFICATION FOCUS

The role and importance of the Church in the worldwide community: how and why it works for reconciliation and the problems faced by the persecuted Church; divergent Christian responses to teachings about charity, including 1 Corinthians 13 and Matthew 25: 31–46; the work of Christian Aid, what it does and why.

> ‘ Wherever we see the Word of God purely preached and heard, there a church of God exists. ’
> *Theologian John Calvin (1509–1564)*

A The world listens to South Africa's Archbishop Desmond Tutu, who was awarded the 1984 Nobel Peace Prize for his key role in fighting against racial discrimination in his homeland

What is reconciliation?

Reconciliation mends broken relationships, bringing peace and harmony between individuals, groups or countries. Today, the Church seeks to reconcile relationships around the world because Jesus taught, 'As I have loved you, so you must love one another' (*John 13: 34*) and because the Bible says:

> ❛All this is from God, who reconciled us to himself through Christ and gave us the ministry of reconciliation. ❜
> *(2 Corinthians 5: 18)*

Have you ever fallen out with someone? Did you make up? What steps were needed in order to 'reconcile' with them?   **SUPPORT**

The Church brings together people of different, and often opposing, beliefs to help them reach a reconciliation. It offers prayer, friendship and advice, as well as financial help and expert practical help in difficult situations. Two examples are the Ecumenical Movement and the World Council of Churches.

Ecumenical Movement

Aims to bring Christians of different and opposing viewpoints together by:

- praying and seeking guidance
- arranging meetings to share viewpoints and situations
- getting churches and groups to work together
- holding conferences and events around the world.

B

World Council of Churches

Seeks reconciliation and peace for people around the world by:

- organising days of prayer
- campaigning for peace and human rights
- responding to calls for help and support
- speaking out against oppression and terrorism
- supporting missionaries.

What is persecution?

Persecution is the ill-treatment of an individual or group, usually on the grounds of religion, politics or ethnicity. Another word for it is **oppression**. Globally, persecution happens on a daily basis. Members or groups within various different faiths have experienced persecution, but a minority who claim allegiance with a particular faith can also be persecutors themselves, often where two different belief systems collide. For example, there is a history of violence between Christian and Muslim groups in Nigeria, with atrocities carried out by both sides.

Do you think that people should always seek reconciliation? Are there some circumstances, such as persecution, where reconciliation seems impossible?   **STRETCH**

Global persecution of Christians is often referred to as 'the persecuted Church', and takes place in many countries, for instance China, North Korea, and India. According to the International Society for Human Rights, 80 per cent of all religious discrimination in the world is currently directed at Christians. It has also been estimated that 100,000 Christians die every year because of their faith.

Former Chief Rabbi Jonathan Sacks told the House of Lords that the persecution of Christians is 'one of the crimes against humanity of our time'. However, very few

C Pakistani Christians mourn after hundreds of people are killed or injured during Easter celebrations in 2016

USEFUL TERMS

Charity: giving to those in need

Persecution: the ill-treatment of an individual or group, usually on the grounds of religion, politics or ethnicity

Reconciliation: restoring peace and friendship between individuals or groups

people in the wealthy countries of 'the West' know about this persecution. One victim said:

> ❛Does anybody hear our cry? How many atrocities must we endure before somebody comes to our aid?❜

Teachings about charity

Christians have a duty to help those in need. This is called **charity**. The Bible says that followers of Jesus must 'love your neighbour as yourself' (*Mark 12: 31*), and that everything they own comes from God and that they look after it for him (see stewardship in 1.2).

> ❛Go, sell everything you have and give it to the poor, and you will have treasure in heaven.❜
> (*Mark 10: 21*)

Although this type of giving is central to Christian teaching, many Christians believe it is especially important to do it quietly. This is because Jesus said:

> ❛Be careful not to practise your righteousness in front of others to be seen by them. If you do, you will have no reward from your Father in heaven [...] [Give your gifts] in secret. Then your Father, who sees what is done in secret, will reward you.❜
> (*Matthew 6: 1, 4*)

D The Salvation Army is an international charitable organisation as well as a Church, whose mission includes 'serving suffering humanity'

St Paul teaches that giving to charity ought to be joyful, and that people should not be forced to give:

> ❝Each of you should give what you have decided in your heart to give, not reluctantly or under compulsion, for God loves a cheerful giver. ❞
> *(2 Corinthians 9: 7)*

One of Jesus' most powerful teachings on charity is the parable of the sheep and goats (*Matthew 25, 31–46*). In it he tells believers that, whenever they give to the poor, they are giving to him:

> ❝... **whatever you did for one of the least of these brothers and sisters of mine, you did for me.** ❞
> *(Matthew 25: 40)*

The most important aspect of Christian charity is love:

> ❝**If I give all I possess to the poor [...] but do not have love, I gain nothing.** ❞
> *(1 Corinthians 13: 3)*

Divergent Christian responses

Christians may respond in a variety of ways to these teachings. Some will give charity and tell no one that they have done it, whereas others will discuss it so as to encourage others to give. Often, Christians will ask God to help them to give joyfully, especially because giving involves a degree of sacrifice and it requires love and compassion. Many Christians will give regular financial gifts to the poor, but giving is not always financial: it can also involve time, effort, and skills dedicated to serving people in need.

Christian Aid

One of the ways believers, and non-believers, can help those in need is to donate to charities like Christian Aid. This is the official relief and development agency of 41 Churches. Much of the money donated to it comes from individual Christians and churches, particularly during Christian Aid Week.

Christian Aid works with local organisations around the world where the need is greatest, regardless of religion or race. It is founded on Christian principles of justice and fairness for all and seeks to obey Jesus' teaching to love one another. Its mission statement is:

> ❝Christian Aid insists the world can and must be swiftly changed to one where everyone can live a full life, free from poverty. ❞

SUPPORT Christians have a profound love and respect for Jesus, and in this teaching he is telling them to treat others with the same respect that they have for him.

STRETCH Why is love so important for Christians giving to charity? Isn't the actual gift the most important thing?

E Christian Aid and partners distributing relief material in the Kathmandu Valley following the Nepal earthquake in May 2015

It aims to help the poor to help themselves and often uses the saying,

> ❝Give a man a fish, feed him for a day; teach a man to fish, feed him for life.❞

Christian Aid operates in three main ways:

- It gives immediate aid such as first aid, food, shelter, and clothing in times of disaster. In 2014, it gave emergency help during the famine in South Sudan and the Ebola disease outbreak in Sierra Leone, and in 2015 after the earthquake in Nepal.
- It gives long-term aid and education to help the poor feed themselves. For example, it has provided medical care, clean water, and farming equipment in many countries, including Ethiopia, Malawi and Afghanistan.
- It runs political campaigns. In 2012, it organised marches in London against climate change and for more provision for the poor.

Christian Aid also works for reconciliation, defends the poor against the rich and powerful, works to end oppressive debt, and campaigns for justice and human rights.

 BUILD YOUR SKILLS

1. Copy and complete the following table for the Church in the worldwide community.

	What does it mean?	How does it impact the Church?
Reconciliation		
Persecution		
Charity		

2. 'Charity begins at home.' Some argue that to give charity and financial aid to overseas countries is wrong when there is poverty and need in the UK.
   a. How would a Christian respond to this and why?
   b. What is your own view?

3. Find out more about the work of Christian Aid. Can you link what they say and do to specific Christian teachings? **STRETCH**

 SUMMARY

- The Christian Church seeks to have a positive impact on the world.
- It preaches the gospel all around the world.
- It helps the needy and tries to influence debate on many global issues.
- It works for reconciliation.
- Many Christians around the world are persecuted for their faith.
- The Bible teaches that Christians must give charity to those in need and Christian Aid is the official Church charity for carrying out that work.

? EXAM-STYLE QUESTIONS

b. Explain **two** ways that Christian Aid works to relieve poverty. (4)

c. Explain **two** reasons why giving to charity is important to Christians. In your answer you must refer to a source of wisdom and authority. (5)

Revision

BUILD YOUR SKILLS

Look at the list of 'I can' statements below and think carefully about how confident you are. Use the following code to rate each of the statements. Be honest!

Green – very confident. What is your evidence for this?

Orange – quite confident. What is your target? Be specific.

Red – not confident. What is your target? Be specific.

A self-assessment revision checklist is available on *Kerboodle*

I can...

- Describe the different ways that Christians worship, including liturgical, non-liturgical and individual, and explain when and why each form might be used

- Explain different Christian attitudes towards liturgical and non-liturgical forms of worship including reference to different denominations

- Explain what sacraments are and why they are important

- Describe the meaning and celebration of baptism and the Eucharist in at least two denominations, including reference to a source of wisdom and authority

- Describe different Christian attitudes towards the use and number of sacraments in Orthodox, Catholic, and Protestant traditions

- Give examples of different kinds of prayer, with reference to a source of wisdom and authority

- Explain when each type of prayer might be used and why

- Describe different Christian attitudes towards the importance of each type of prayer for Christians today

- Explain what pilgrimage is and why people go on pilgrimages

- Describe the activities associated with different Christian pilgrimages

- Explain different Christian teachings about whether pilgrimage is important for Christians today, with reference to Catholic and Protestant understandings

- Explain the origins and importance of Advent and Christmas

- Explain the origins and importance of Holy Week and Easter, with reference to a source of wisdom and authority

- Explain the meaning of the terms mission and evangelism

- Explain the history and purpose of missionary and evangelistic work in the Church, with reference to a source of wisdom and authority

- Describe some different ways that this work is put into practice by the Church

- Describe Christian attitudes to why evangelistic work is important for the Church and individual Christians

- Explain what the local church does in the local community and why, including reference to a source of wisdom and authority

- Describe the impact the local church has on the individual believer and the local area

- Explain the role and importance of the Church in the worldwide community

- Explain why the Church works for reconciliation

- Describe the problems faced by the persecuted Church

- Give different Christian responses to teachings about charity, with reference to a source of wisdom and authority

- Describe the work of Christian Aid – what it does and why.

Exam practice

On these exam practice pages you will see example answers for each of the exam question types: **a**, **b**, **c**, and **d**. You can find out more about these on pages 6–11.

• Question 'a'

*Question **a** is AO1 – this tests your knowledge and understanding.*

> (a) Outline **three** Christian sacraments. (3)

Student response

Baptism, bread and wine, becoming a priest

Improved student response

Baptism, formally becoming a member of the Christian Church.

Eucharist, a re-enactment of the last supper.

Holy Orders, becoming a priest, deacon or bishop in Catholic and Orthodox Churches.

 Over to you! Give yourself three minutes on the clock and have a go at answering this question. Remember, this question type requires you to provide three facts or short ideas: you don't need to explain them or express any opinions.

 ✓ WHAT WENT WELL

This student can identify three different types of sacrament.

! HOW TO IMPROVE

To make the response clearer and gain full marks the student should use the religious names for the sacraments and explain each one. See the 'improved student response' opposite for suggested corrections.

• Question 'b'

*Question **b** is AO1 – this tests your knowledge and understanding.*

> (b) Explain **two** reasons why prayer is important to Christians. (4)

Student response

Prayer is important to Christians because it is a way of communicating with God. People can pray for different things, for example, to ask for something.

Improved student response

Prayer is important to Christians because it is a way of communicating with God. Through prayer Christians can give thanks and praise to God but also ask for things on behalf of themselves or others.

Prayer is important to Christians because Jesus taught people to pray using the Lord's Prayer and people like to follow his example. In addition, using formal prayers or words from Church history help Christians to feel a shared sense of belief and unity making this form of prayer important for Christians.

 Over to you! Give yourself four minutes on the clock and have a go at answering this question. Remember, in order to 'explain' something, you need to **develop** your points. See page 9 for a reminder of how to do this.

 ✓ WHAT WENT WELL

This is a low-level response with two vague and basic reasons given. The student correctly identifies that prayer is a way of communicating with God.

 ! HOW TO IMPROVE

The reasons given are basic and are not developed. For a high level response students should explain why prayer is important to individual Christians, using examples of how they pray and the types of prayer they use. See the 'improved student response' opposite for suggested corrections.

• Question 'c'

*Question **c** is AO1 – this tests your knowledge and understanding.*

(c) Explain **two** reasons why giving to charity is important to Christians. In your answer you must refer to a source of wisdom and authority. (5)

Student response

The Bible says that Christians must give charity to those in need. Supporting charities is a good thing and the Christian Church seeks to have a positive impact on the world.

Improved student response

Giving to charity is important to Christians because the Bible says that Christians must give charity to those in need. In Jesus' teaching of the parable of the sheep and the goats Jesus says that if we help others, in fact we are helping him, showing that charity to others is important: "whatever you did for one of the least of these brothers and sisters of mine, you did for me" (Matthew 25: 40).

Secondly, Christians are taught that the most charitable act is love and often Christians do not give financially to charity but will give time, effort and skills because supporting charities is a good thing and the Christian Church seeks to have a positive impact on the world.

 Over to you! Give yourself five minutes on the clock and have a go at answering this question. Remember, you need to write two developed points, one of which needs to be supported by a source of wisdom and authority.

 ✓ WHAT WENT WELL

This student understands that charity is important and the global Church has a responsibility to help others.

 ❗ HOW TO IMPROVE

The link between helping others by giving to charity and Christian teachings on charity could be clearer. Has the student included a source of wisdom and authority? See the 'improved student response' opposite for suggested corrections.

• Question 'd'

*Question **d** is AO2 – this tests your ability to evaluate. Some 'd' questions also carry an extra three marks for spelling, punctuation and grammar.*

In this question, 3 of the marks awarded will be for your spelling, punctuation and grammar and your use of specialist terminology.

*(d) 'Every Christian should go on a pilgrimage.' Evaluate this statement considering arguments for and against. In your response you should:
- refer to Christian teachings
- refer to different Christian points of view
- reach a justified conclusion. (15)

Student response

Christians have been going on <u>pilgrimiges</u> for centuries, and today <u>pilgrimige</u> is still popular. <u>Pilgrimige</u> can increase a Christian's faith, help them feel closer to God, and may bring about religious experiences.

I would agree with the claim that every Christian should go on a <u>pilgrimige</u>, because it's a spiritual journey towards God. Many popular sites of <u>pilgrimige</u> –

for instance Jerusalem – are visited by Christians and it could be argued that Christians should go to Jerusalem because Jesus himself did this.

However, not all Christians place emphasis on <u>pilgrimige</u>. It might be encouraged as a special opportunity to pray and reflect, but it's not considered to be central to living the Christian life. These Christians might choose to focus on other aspects of their faith instead.

In conclusion, whilst <u>pilgrimige</u> would be very beneficial to all Christians, it's not possible to say that all Christians should go on a <u>pilgrimige</u>. It's not a religious requirement, and in some churches it's not a significant part of the Christian life.

Improved student response

Christians have been going on <u>pilgrimages</u> for centuries, and today pilgrimage is still popular. Pilgrimage can increase a Christian's faith, help them feel closer to God, and may bring about religious experiences.

A member of the Catholic Church could agree with the claim that every Christian should go on a pilgrimage, because the Catholic Church teaches about its importance in the Catechism: 'Pilgrimages evoke our earthly journey toward heaven' (CCC 2691). In other words, pilgrimage is a spiritual journey towards God.

Pilgrimage is important in Protestant churches too, and many popular sites of pilgrimage – for instance Jerusalem and Walsingham – are visited by all denominations. Walsingham, for instance, has Catholic, Anglican, and Orthodox shrines. It could be argued that all Christians should go on a pilgrimage to Jerusalem because Jesus himself did this at the age of twelve and said that he had to be in his Father's house (Luke 2: 49). Pilgrimage can allow Christians to walk in the very footsteps of Jesus, or a saint. Pilgrimage is spiritually important because the pilgrim can, for a moment, be where Jesus or a saint was, see what they saw, and experience what the world was like for them – it makes it special for the pilgrim and something which they will never forget.

However, not all Protestant churches place emphasis on pilgrimage. It might be encouraged as a special opportunity to pray and reflect, but it's not considered to be central to living the Christian life. These Christians might choose to focus on other aspects of their faith instead, for example prayer, Bible study or evangelism – all of which bring Christians closer to God in an everyday way which fits into their lives.

In conclusion, whilst pilgrimage would be very beneficial to all Christians, it's not possible to say that all Christians should go on a pilgrimage. It's not a religious requirement, and in some churches it's not a significant part of the Christian life.

 Over to you! Give yourself 15 minutes on the clock and have a go at answering this question. Remember to refer back to the original statement in your writing when you give different points of view, and make sure you cover each of the bullet points given in the question. Allow three minutes to check your spelling, punctuation and grammar and use of specialist terminology.

 WHAT WENT WELL

This is a mid-level response. The student understands that they must give two opposing sides of the argument and reach a conclusion. They explain both arguments and present a conclusion.

 HOW TO IMPROVE

This student has consistently misspelt the word 'pilgrimage', which would cost them marks. To achieve a high-level answer, the student would need to be more specific when referring to different Christian viewpoints, and provide more detail on Christian teachings. See the 'improved student response' opposite for suggested corrections.

 BUILD YOUR SKILLS

In your exams, you'll need to make sure you use religious terminology correctly. Do you know the meaning of the following important terms for this topic?

worship · liturgical · non-liturgical · prejudice · pilgrimage · Advent · Holy Week · mission · evangelism · ecumenism · persecution

Chapter 4:

Peace and Conflict

What are Christian attitudes to peace?

Most Christians believe that they should work towards establishing a peaceful world and ending war, because the sixth of the Ten Commandments forbids killing people, and because Jesus encouraged his followers to seek peace, reconciliation, and **forgiveness**. Jesus stopped his disciples from using violence; for example he told Peter to put away his sword when he had drawn it to fight the soldiers coming to arrest him (*Matthew 26: 52*).

Some of Jesus' most well-known teachings relate to peace:

- 'Blessed are the peacemakers, for they shall be called children of God.' (*Matthew 5: 9*).
- 'do not resist an evil person. If anyone slaps you on the right cheek, turn to them the other cheek also.' (*Matthew 5: 39*).
- 'love your enemies and pray for those who persecute you' (*Matthew 5: 44*).
- 'all who draw the sword will die by the sword.' (*Matthew 26: 52*).

For many Christians, these teachings mean that they should not engage in conflict and wars (see 4.3). For several centuries after the death of Christ, the early Christians refused to fight in wars. Today, many Christians are **pacifists**, and feel that war can never be justified. They believe that they should be **peacemakers** instead, working for peace and not war, as Jesus commanded.

> ❝ But love your enemies, do good to them, and lend to them without expecting to get anything back. Then your reward will be great, and you will be children of the Most High [...] be merciful, just as your Father is merciful. ❞
> (*Luke 6: 35–36*)

However, other Christians believe that it is sometimes necessary to fight, for example to protect innocent people from a brutal enemy. They see fighting as the 'lesser of two evils', and would highlight the fact that the Bible contains examples of good people taking up arms, particularly in the Old Testament.

In the Bible, Paul also says that people must obey their governments:

> ❝ Let everyone be subject to the governing authorities, for there is no authority except that which God has established. ❞
> (*Romans 13: 1*)

Some Christians interpret these instructions as meaning that people may sometimes have to obey an order to fight in a war.

SPECIFICATION FOCUS

Christian attitudes towards peace: divergent Christian attitudes towards the nature and importance of peace for Christians; Church teachings about peace, including Jesus as a peacemaker including interpretations of Luke 22: 47–53.

USEFUL TERMS

Conscientious objector: someone who refuses to serve in the armed forces for ethical reasons

Forgiveness: pardoning a person for a wrong committed against you; in a Christian context, forgiveness doesn't always come about because the person deserves to be forgiven, but out of love, mercy, and grace

Pacifist: someone who believes that war and violence are never justified

Peacemaker: someone who works for peace and an end to conflict

A British soldiers worshipping in a damaged church in northern France during the First World War

What does the Church teach about peace?

Churches have tried to encourage peace in the world and to encourage all Christians to seek peace and not war. In many conflicts, **conscientious objectors**, including some Christians (for example Quakers), have refused to fight. However, as the Bible does not explicitly state whether or not Christians should fight in a war, many Christians believe that, in certain circumstances, it may be right to fight – for example, in a so-called Just War (see 4.5). This view is supported by several denominations – Catholic, Anglican, Methodist, Baptist, and the United Reformed Church.

Jesus as a peacemaker

Luke's gospel says that, when Jesus was arrested, the soldiers had been led by one of his own disciples – Judas Iscariot. Judas was about to greet Jesus when Jesus said: 'Judas, are you betraying the Son of Man with a kiss?' (*Luke 22: 48*). Jesus told his followers not to fight the soldiers – he wanted peace, not bloodshed. He healed a man whose ear had already been wounded, and told his enemies that he presented no threat to them. He said that everything was in God's hands and that the final battle against evil was still to come.

B The arrest of Jesus and Judas' kiss, shown in a fresco in the Convent of San Marco, Italy

> '**Am I leading a rebellion, that you have come with swords and clubs?** Every day I was with you in the temple courts, and you did not lay a hand on me. But this is your hour – when darkness reigns. '
> (*Luke 22: 52–53*)

Interpretations

- Many Christians interpret this as a teaching not to engage in conflict, but to trust in God instead.
- Others, however, think that it shows that they should not engage in petty, personal incidents of violence, but that it does not apply to larger-scale warfare.
- Some Christians see it as a far more specific instruction that Jesus did not want his disciples to defend him because he knew he needed to go to the cross.

'Peace' features strongly in the teachings of Jesus, but it is clear that his teachings on peace are not explicitly about not going to war. Instead they are to do with internal peace that he encourages all his followers to attain – an inner peace of mind and spirit.

BUILD YOUR SKILLS

1. Christians often refer to Jesus as the 'Prince of Peace' (*Isaiah 9: 6*). Why do you think this is? Refer to Jesus' teachings in your answer.

2. Look at image **A**. How does this image illustrate the dilemma faced by Christians who are asked to go to war?

3. Can a God of peace ask his followers to serve in the armed forces? Write arguments for and against, and reach a justified conclusion. **STRETCH**

SUMMARY

- Jesus was a peacemaker and taught about the importance of responding peacefully in times of conflict.
- Many Christians believe that they should be peacemakers and should not fight in a conflict.
- Some Christians will fight for a cause, such as stopping others getting hurt.

EXAM-STYLE QUESTIONS

a. Outline **three** Christian beliefs about peace. (3)

b. Explain **two** reasons why a Christian might choose not to fight in a war. (4)

What does Christianity teach about peacemaking?

In the Sermon on the Mount, Jesus taught his followers about the importance of peacemaking:

> '**Blessed are the peacemakers**, for they will be called children of God. '
> *(Matthew 5: 9)*

Jesus taught that his followers should always seek to make peace:

> 'Love your enemies and pray for those who persecute you [...] if you love those who love you, what reward will you get? [...] Be perfect, therefore, as your heavenly Father is perfect. '
> *(Matthew 5: 44–48)*

All ancient documents, the Bible included, have a historical context. Jesus taught at the time the Roman Empire was reaching its peak. Rome had conquered much of the known world, and it did so because the Romans felt their role was to establish universal peace. However, their way of establishing this peace was by killing all who opposed them. Jesus' way of establishing peace, as demonstrated throughout the gospels, was one of forgiveness, reconciliation, and grace. Instructions to love your enemies, and to pray for people who persecute you, would have seemed a radical contrast to Roman ideas.

Justice, forgiveness and reconciliation

For Christians, **justice**, forgiveness, and reconciliation are particularly important in peacemaking because of Jesus' teachings. Jesus modelled reconciliation – the restoring of relationships between people. He taught forgiveness and love of one's enemies (see 4.1).

For Christians, it is important to stress that real peace cannot be achieved without justice first. Peace doesn't mean that Christians ignore injustice for the sake of avoiding conflict. Real peace, a Christian would argue, is only possible if injustices have been repaired first. The Catholic Church teaches that true peace will only be achieved if the inequalities between people and nations which lead to war are fixed. In the Second Vatican Council, the Catholic bishops said: '…peace on earth can never be achieved unless every person's well-being is safeguarded'.

SPECIFICATION FOCUS

The role of Christians in peacemaking: Christian teachings about peacemaking; the importance of justice, forgiveness and reconciliation for Christians in peacemaking; the work of one Christian group working for peace today, what it does and why it tries to work for peace, including Matthew 5: 1–16.

USEFUL TERMS

Apartheid: system in South Africa which segregated and discriminated against people according to their race

Justice: doing what is right and fair based on the law

A A stained glass window showing the Sermon on the Mount

How do Christian groups work for peace?

A number of groups campaign in non-violent ways for world peace. They do this by:

- encouraging opposing sides to talk to each other to achieve reconciliation
- campaigning against oppressive governments
- keeping people informed of injustices around the world
- encouraging non-violent protest.

CASE STUDY: CHRISTIAN ORGANISATIONS

World Council of Churches

World Council of Churches **B**

World Council of Churches (WCC) brings together Christians from all over the world. It works for world peace by arranging for those in disputes, particularly religious ones, to talk to each other, in order to sort things out and achieve reconciliation.

In its Programme to Combat Racism, the WCC worked for peace and justice in the struggle against **apartheid** in South Africa. It has also been involved in conflicts in Sudan, Korea and Latin America.

Pax Christi

Pax Christi (Latin for 'Peace of Christ') is an international Catholic peace movement, set up in 1945. Pax Christi is opposed to war and violence and tries to get governments to solve their disputes with other nations through talking, and through economic and social justice.

PAX CHRISTI
International Catholic Movement for Peace **C**

The work of Pax Christi is based on the gospel and inspired by faith. Pax Christi believes that peace is possible and that vicious cycles of violence and injustice can be broken. Our vision is of a world where people can live in peace, free from the fear of violence in all its forms.
(Pax Christi website, www. paxchristi.org.uk)

D A small peace vigil held by Pax Christi in London 2015 to remember the victims of the Hiroshima and Nagasaki atomic bombs (see 4.7)

BUILD YOUR SKILLS

1. Why are 'justice' and 'reconciliation' so important to Christians? Use Christian teachings in your answer.

2. How do Christian organisations work for peace? Give examples. Do you think this work is successful?

3. 'Love your friends and hate your enemies.' Is this good or bad advice? Why? What would a Christian argue?

SUMMARY

- Jesus taught that his followers must seek and work for peace.
- This view is supported in the work of many Christian churches and groups.

? EXAM-STYLE QUESTIONS

b Explain **two** reasons why Christians believe that peacemaking is important. (4)

d 'There can never be peace in this world.'
Evaluate this statement considering arguments for and against. In your argument you should:
- refer to Christian teachings
- reach a justified conclusion. (12)

4.3 Conflict

SPECIFICATION FOCUS

Christian attitudes to conflict: Christian teachings and responses to the nature and causes of conflict; Christian responses to the problems conflict causes, including Matthew 26: 47–56 and links to situation ethics; non-religious (including atheist and Humanist) attitudes about the role of religion in the causes of conflict and Christian responses to them.

What causes conflict?

Conflict is not always violent. Often, issues within a nation or between nations can be resolved through political negotiation and compromise. However, an armed conflict between two or more nations is known as war. The causes of war are often concerned with either protecting a nation's way of life or improving that way of life. There are several main factors that can lead to this kind of conflict.

self-defence · economics · environment/natural resources

A Causes of conflict

fear · national pride · religion · long-standing racial or ethnic hatred

CASE STUDY: THE IRAQ WAR

The Iraq War provides an example of how these different factors can operate. It began on 20 March 2003, when armed forces from several countries, led by the US, launched an attack against Iraq. The aim, according to US President George W. Bush, was 'to disarm Iraq, to free its people, and to defend the world from grave danger'.

Factor 1: fear
Many people believed that Iraqi leader Saddam Hussein had weapons of mass destruction that were a threat to the western world.

Factor 2: national pride
The US believed that Saddam Hussein had links with terrorist networks, who had been responsible for terrorist attacks such as the World Trade Center in 2001 (see image **D**). Some felt that the US should punish Iraq and restore US national pride.

Factor 3: economics
The countries involved wanted access to Iraq's large oil supplies, which are vital to the Western economy.

The war began with a missile attack on Saddam Hussein's headquarters, and soon after, armed forces seized the Iraq oilfields. The conflict lasted just a few weeks. By 8 April, troops had surrounded Baghdad. Saddam Hussein fled.

Although most Iraqis seemed pleased to see the end of Saddam Hussein's rule, small groups continued to fight. There was widespread violence and looting, and the armed forces faced the huge task of restoring law and order.

Meanwhile, worldwide criticism against the war grew, particularly because no weapons of mass destruction had been found. President Bush and UK Prime Minister Tony Blair came under great pressure to remove their troops from Iraq.

B The bombing of the Iraqi city of Baghdad during the Iraq War, March 2003

C Many people took part in demonstrations against the UK's involvement in the Iraq War

How do Christians respond to conflict?

Christians believe in working towards world peace. However, they may approach this in different ways:

- **Belief in pacifism (see 4.4):** pacifists believe that war can never be justified. Some Christians will not get involved in any kind of violence. They believe that disputes can always be solved peacefully, in accordance with the teachings of Jesus. Christian pacifist groups include the Quakers and the Plymouth Brethren.

- **Belief in Just War (see 4.5):** some Christians believe that it may be right to fight in some circumstances, for example to protect the innocent from an aggressive enemy. Christian churches that support this viewpoint include Catholics, Anglicans, Methodists, and Baptists.

- **Dealing with the cause:** whether a Christian is a pacifist or a supporter of just war, all Christians recognise that often the cause of conflict is something else which needs to be fixed before the conflict can be ended. For example, injustice and inequality can lead to conflict, and would need to be dealt with before the conflict can truly be resolved.

Jesus' attitude to conflict

When Jesus was arrested after his betrayal by Judas Iscariot, one of his disciples, he did not resist those coming to arrest him (*Matthew 26: 47–56*). Jesus told his followers to put their swords down and not fight because 'all who draw the sword will die by the sword' (*Matthew 26: 52*). For many Christians, this teaching means that fighting simply creates more problems, rather than solving anything. They believe they should follow Jesus' example of trusting that everything is in God's control, and that there is no need for violence.

However, some Christians interpret the teaching differently (see 4.1). They say the teaching:

- is a specific situation because Jesus knew he had to go to the cross. He wasn't necessarily discouraging all forms of violence.

- refers only to small-scale personal conflicts and does not give guidance on full-scale war.

Links to situation ethics

Situation ethics is the ethical theory that moral decisions should be based on what is the most loving thing to do, depending on the particular situation. The theory:

- judges every situation individually
- rejects fixed rules
- evaluates situations with the principle of love.

Situation ethics allows a person to weigh up a situation and exercise some choice over what to do, rather than just following a rule without question. Going to war or killing an enemy could be the most loving thing to do in certain circumstances. For example, the most loving thing might be to kill a person who was about to detonate a nuclear bomb that would kill thousands.

D The terrorist attack on the World Trade Center, New York, 11 September 2001, in which nearly 3000 people died

> Read and make notes on *Matthew 26: 47–56*. What do you think Jesus means when he says 'all who draw the sword will die by the sword'? Which of the main Christian interpretations of this passage do you agree with most, and why? **STRETCH**

However, many Christians disagree with the situation ethics approach because:

- an individual's view of what is the most loving thing to do can be extremely subjective
- it is not possible to know how the future might turn out
- murder could be justified as 'the most loving thing'
- they believe that fixed rules offer a more consistent and fair solution.

Those who oppose situation ethics say that it is impossible to know what is the most loving thing to do in every situation.

What non-religious viewpoints are there about conflict?

Some non-religious people, including atheists and Humanists, believe that religion is a major factor in causing wars, for example:

- the Crusades in medieval times (see 4.6)
- conflicts between Protestants and Catholics in Ireland
- the conflict between Christians and Muslims in Bosnia and Serbia in the 1990s
- conflicts between Muslims and Hindus in Kashmir
- conflicts between religious groups in the Middle East.

Some people believe that if religion was abolished, there would be less conflict and fewer wars.

E In the Crusades, Christians from Western Europe fought Muslims to take control of Jerusalem; this Christian engraving shows Christian soldiers fighting an Egyptian army in 1099CE

> ❝Many Humanists do not believe that religion ever provides an appropriate motive for war. Any 'holy war' fought purely for the achievement of some religious goal, or motivated by some notion of a spiritual reward for those who take part, is likely to be disapproved of by Humanists.❞
> (British Humanist Association)

Can you explain this argument in your own words?

SUPPORT

As Humanists use the guiding principle of not harming others, they assess which course of action is likely to cause least harm:

> ❝We should always seek non-violent solutions first [...] However terrible war may be, it's at least possible that sometimes a refusal to go to war may be even worse [...] if Nazism had not been resisted there might have been an even worse outcome.❞
> (British Humanist Association)

Christian responses to non-religious viewpoints about the role of religion in conflict

In response to the assertion that religion is a major factor in causing war, some Christians argue that:

- often what seems to be a religious dispute is actually about culture and social belief
- all religions call for peace
- Christianity teaches people to love their enemies
- some people misinterpret religious teaching.

It is clear that religion has been used to justify war, even if behind the justification there are other motivations. People can often be persuaded to commit **atrocities** if they can be convinced they are doing it for a higher power, such as God. In 2004, Archbishop Michael Fitzgerald wrote in *The Times*:

> 'There is hardly a conflict today [...] without a religious dimension [...] I think religious differences are used to set people against each other. Religion isn't usually the cause of the conflict, but it's an added factor. '
> *(The Times)*

USEFUL TERMS

Atrocity: extremely cruel or barbaric attack, usually involving violence

Conflict: a serious disagreement

Looting: stealing goods from shops and houses, usually during a war or a riot

Pacifism: the belief that war can never be justified and that conflicts should be settled peacefully

Situation ethics: ethical decisions are made according to the specific context of the decision

Terrorist: person who uses unlawful violence or threats to harm or injure people

BUILD YOUR SKILLS

1. Look at diagram **A**. Choose two of the factors that cause war and write a sentence of explanation for each one.

2. Read the **case study** on page 114.
   a. In your opinion, which of the three factors that caused the Iraq War is the most justifiable, and which is the least? Explain your reasons.
   b. How would different Christians have responded to this war? Explain your answer.

3. Copy and complete the following table:

Does religion cause conflict?			
Arguments 'for'	Strengths/ weaknesses of the argument	Arguments 'against'	Strengths/ weaknesses of the argument
Yes, because...		No, because...	

SUMMARY

- Many Christians believe that the Bible tells people not to engage in war.
- Other Christians believe that under certain circumstances, going to war is the right thing to do.
- Many Humanists believe that people should try to find peaceful solutions to conflicts, but that sometimes going to war may avoid greater harm.

EXAM-STYLE QUESTIONS

a. Outline **three** causes of war. (3)
b. Explain **two** reasons why a non-religious person could argue that religion causes war. (4)

4.4 Pacifism

What does Christianity teach about pacifism?

Pacifism is the belief that violence and war cannot be justified, and that conflicts should be settled peacefully. There are key biblical teachings that might lead a Christian to choose pacifism:

- The Ten Commandments forbid killing: 'You shall not murder' (*Exodus 20: 13*).
- Jesus taught that people should love their enemies (*Matthew 5: 44*).
- Jesus stopped his own followers from using violence (*Matthew 26: 52*).

A number of Christian groups, such as the Quakers, the Plymouth Brethren, and Pax Christi do not engage in any kind of violent struggle and state that they will not resist those who attack them.

Quakers were one of the first Christian groups to adopt pacifism. In 1660, its members made a commitment never to fight or serve in the army. Soon afterwards, Quakers declared to King Charles II:

> ❛... the Spirit of Christ, which leads us into all truth, will never move us to fight and war against any person with outward weapons. ❜
> *(Quaker declaration to Charles II and parliament, 1660)*

Today, Quakers offer to act as **mediators** for peace and do peace-giving acts, such as supporting people in need.

However, many Christians oppose pacifism because they would argue:

- **aggressors** always win
- there is nobody prepared to fight for others or protect the innocent
- evil can flourish over good.

Some Christian organisations believe that it is legitimate for countries to go to war if there is good reason:

> ❛All citizens and all governments are obliged to work for the avoidance of war. However [...] governments cannot be denied the right of lawful self-defence, once all peace efforts have failed. ❜
> *(Catechism of the Catholic Church, 2308)*

SPECIFICATION FOCUS

Christian attitudes to pacifism: divergent Christian teachings and responses to the nature and history of pacifism, including reference to Quakers; divergent Christian teachings about passive resistance, including John 14: 22–31 and an example of its use, including Martin Luther King.

USEFUL TERMS

Aggressor: person, group or country that is the first to attack another

Mediator: person who tries to help those in conflict reach agreement

Passive resistance: non-violent opposition to something; this may involve going against certain laws

A Quakers promote peace and oppose war

What does Christianity teach about passive resistance?

CASE STUDY: MARTIN LUTHER KING JR

Many Christians have been inspired by Christian minister Dr Martin Luther King Jr. He believed that God was on the side of poor and oppressed people, and he dedicated his life to working for equal rights for black people in the US. Dr King promoted passive resistance, and organised non-violent demonstrations to persuade the government to grant equal rights to all people. For example, King led the Montgomery bus boycott of 1955–1956 following the arrest of Rosa Parks, an African American woman who was arrested because she did not give up her seat on a bus for a white man. Though King was imprisoned for two weeks, the boycott was successful and brought about greater equality on US public transport. In 1964, he won the Nobel Peace Prize and, thanks to his work, black Americans secured voting rights in 1965. He was assassinated by James Earl Ray in 1968.

 B King speaking about his arrest following the bus boycott; his arrest raised the profile of the boycott to the national stage

Throughout the four Gospels, Jesus is an example of passive resistance for Christians. His teachings were radical: for example, rather than hating enemies, he taught that people should love and even pray for them (*Matthew 5: 44*), and he discouraged revenge even when it seems to be justified (*Matthew 5: 39*).

Christians do not interpret these teachings to mean that they should simply be passive. For example, Martin Luther King Jr managed to resist racism on a large scale, without violence (see **case study**). For Christians, Jesus' example is one that can powerfully change things for the better. This is particularly demonstrated through the death of Jesus on the cross. Jesus said the following to his disciples:

> ‘I will not say much more to you, for **the prince of this world is coming. He has no hold over me**, but he comes so that the world may learn that I love the Father and do exactly what my Father has commanded me.’
> (*John 14: 30–31*)

Here Jesus is predicting the evil that will come to destroy him, but that ultimately it will be beaten. In not resisting his arrest and crucifixion, Christians believe Jesus won a great victory over evil in his resurrection.

BUILD YOUR SKILLS

1 Write a short explanation for the following words: pacifism, Quaker, passive resistance. **SUPPORT**

2 Create a list of Christian arguments for and against violent action. Which argument is the strongest, and which is the weakest? Explain your conclusions.

3 'Passive resistance is the best way to resolve conflict.' Using your arguments from Activity **2**, write a response to this statement. Refer to Martin Luther King Jr in your response.

SUMMARY

- Christians are required by the Bible to seek peace with their enemies.
- Churches have differing views on whether a Christian may fight.
- Today many Christians are pacifists, including Quakers.

EXAM-STYLE QUESTIONS

a Outline **three** Christian beliefs about pacifism. (3)

d 'Pacifism only allows aggressors to win.' Evaluate this statement considering arguments for and against. In your argument you should:
- refer to Christian teachings
- refer to different Christian points of view
- reach a justified conclusion. (12)

4.5 Just war

What is the Just War theory?

St Augustine, a fifth-century bishop, suggested that religious believers should fight in a conflict only if certain conditions were met. These conditions were developed in the thirteenth century by Thomas Aquinas and collectively are known as the **Just War theory**.

> ❛... they who have waged war in obedience to the divine command, or in conformity with His laws, have represented in their persons the public justice or the wisdom of government, and in this capacity have put to death wicked men; such persons have by no means violated the commandment, "You shall not kill." ❜
> *(St Augustine)*

What are the conditions for a just war?

According to the Just War theory, the conditions that have to be met for Christians to go to war are as follows:

- The cause of the war is just, meaning that it is morally right and fair, such as resisting aggression and injustice.
- The war is fought with the authority of the government or United Nations.
- The war is fought with the intention of bringing peace.
- The decision to go to war is a last resort after all non-violent methods of solving the conflict have failed.
- There is a reasonable likelihood of success.
- Warfare must be careful and civilians should not be targeted.
- The methods used must be reasonably proportionate between the injustice being fought and the suffering that is inflicted.

Problems with the Just War theory

The main problem with the Just War theory is that both sides in a war may claim that their cause is just. Leaders can also justify their actions by claiming that what they have done is God's will. For instance, after the invasion of Iraq, US President George W. Bush reputedly declared, 'God told me to strike at al-Qaeda and I struck them, and then he instructed me to strike at Saddam, which I did.' President Bush also said, 'This will be a monumental struggle of good versus evil, but good will prevail' and described America's enemies as the 'axis of evil'.

SPECIFICATION FOCUS

Christian attitudes to the Just War theory: Christian teachings and responses to the nature, history and importance of the Just War theory; the conditions of a just war; divergent Christian opinions about whether a just war is possible, including Romans 13: 1–7, including the application of ethical theories such as situation ethics.

A St Augustine

What does Christianity teach about the Just War theory?

Many Christians believe that God will support just wars, and there are biblical teachings in line with this.

Bible passage	What it teaches
'Praise be to the Lord my Rock, who trains my hands for war' (Psalm 144: 1)	In the Old Testament, God is sometimes described as supporting those in battle
'Let everyone be subject to the governing authorities, for there is no authority except that which God has established [...] if you do wrong, be afraid, for **rulers do not bear the sword for no reason. They are God's servants**, agents of wrath to bring punishment on the wrongdoer.' (Romans 13: 1, 4)	Paul said that Christians have a duty to obey those in authority and respect a ruler's right to punish others
'if you don't have a sword, sell your cloak and buy one' (Luke 22: 36)	Jesus seems to be encouraging the use of weapons – at least in self-defence
'Greater love has no one than this: to lay down one's life for one's friends' (John 15: 13)	Jesus makes it clear that being willing to die for another is the highest form of love

Some Christians also claim that, just as a police force protects citizens from criminals, so it is right to have armed forces to protect a nation from enemies:

'In choosing whether or not to take up arms, every Christian must weigh up the potential cost against the need to protect those who cannot protect themselves and [to] oppose the tyrants and dictators who can only be stopped by force. If the Christian will not take up the challenge, who will? (Peter Lee, King's College London)

However, some Christians do not accept the Just War theory because:
- they believe that God does not support war in any form
- it is possible for both sides to claim that their cause is just
- Romans 13: 1–7 was not intended to justify the wielding of power, it's more about being a good citizen.

'... in this age which boasts of its atomic power, it no longer makes sense to maintain that war is a fit instrument with which to repair the violation of justice. (Pope John XXIII)

B George W. Bush, US President 2001–09

USEFUL TERM

Just War theory: a set of conditions that need to be met in order for a war to be justified

C Pope John XXIII

121

How do situation ethics relate to the Just War theory?

Supporters of situation ethics (see 4.3) do not necessarily accept the Just War theory:

- They would argue that it is only right to fight a war if it is the most loving thing to do.

- However, as war is so complex it may be impossible to know what the most loving thing to do actually is.

- There is also the problem that both sides may claim that they are doing the most loving thing.

BUILD YOUR SKILLS

1   You'll need to be able to remember the conditions of the Just War theory (page 120). For each one, draw a symbol or choose a word which will help you to remember it. Ask a partner to test you using your symbols/words. **SUPPORT**

2   a   Create a scenario in which a ruler wants to attack another nation. Decide:
- why your ruler wants to go to war
- what other attempts the ruler has made to resolve the conflict
- what methods would be used to win the attack.

   b   In pairs, use the list of conditions for a just war on page 120 to evaluate your scenarios. Are your wars just? Which conditions, if any, have you broken?

3   Why do some Christians disagree about the Just War theory? Refer to Christian teachings in your answer.

4   Does the fact that both sides of a conflict can claim to be fighting a just war make the theory a failure? Why or why not? **STRETCH**

SUMMARY

- The Just War theory is a set of conditions that need to be met in order for a war to be justified.
- Some Christians believe the theory is supported by biblical teachings.
- Other Christians disagree and do not accept the Just War theory.
- Sometimes skilful leaders use and distort the Just War theory in order to gain support for their actions.

? EXAM-STYLE QUESTIONS

b   Explain **two** conditions of the Just War theory. (4)

c   Explain **two** reasons why the Just War theory is important for Christians. In your answer you must refer to a source of wisdom and authority. (5)

4.6 Holy war

What is a holy war?

A **holy war** is one in which religion is the driving force. It has three elements:

- its aim is the achievement of a religious outcome
- it is authorised by a religious leader
- there is a spiritual reward for those who take part.

A holy war is not the same as a just war. Instead, it has five unique aims.

to spread the faith

to convert countries to a different religious faith

to rescue religious believers from non-believing countries

A Aims of a holy war

to save and restore religious and sacred places that the enemy are destroying

to take revenge against blasphemies and cruelties against believers

What does Christianity teach about holy war?

In the Old Testament there are many examples of holy wars. In the book of Joshua, chapter 6, God commands Joshua, as the leader of Israel's armies, to take the city of Jericho. In the Book of Psalms, David expresses his gratitude to God for helping him defeat enemies who attacked the people of Israel (see *Psalm 144*).

Jesus' teaching in *Matthew 10: 34–40*

In Matthew's gospel, Jesus appears to call on his disciples to take up arms. Some Christians would interpret this to mean that Jesus expects to cause conflict:

> ❝Do not suppose that I have come to bring peace to the earth. **I did not come to bring peace, but a sword**. For I have come to turn a man against his father, a daughter against her mother [...] a man's enemies will be the members of his own household [...] anyone who loves his father or mother more than me is not worthy of me [...] whoever does not take up his cross and follow me is not worthy of me. Whoever finds their life will lose it, and whoever loses their life for my sake will find it. ❞
> *(Matthew 10: 34–39)*

B God commanded Joshua to encircle the walled city of Jericho before attacking; this was a holy war

---

SPECIFICATION FOCUS

Christian attitudes to Holy War: Christian teachings and responses to the nature of a holy war; the nature and meaning of teachings about war and peace as shown in the Bible, including Matthew 10: 34–40; divergent Christian teachings about war; non-religious (including atheist and Humanist) attitudes towards holy war and Christian responses to them.

USEFUL TERM

Holy war: war to spread a religious belief or to defend that belief

However, other Christians believe that Jesus is not calling out for war, but is talking about a spiritual 'sword' which may need to cut family ties in favour of a more important spiritual responsibility. This would enable a Christian to concentrate on following Jesus, rather than family, and the reward would be eternal life. These Christians believe that the real holy war is a spiritual war against the powers of evil, involving 'spiritual' weapons and defences rather than actual weapons:

> ❝Put on the full armour of God, so that you can take your stand against the devil's schemes. For our struggle is not against flesh and blood, but against [...] the powers of this dark world and against the spiritual forces of evil in the heavenly realms. ❞
> *(Ephesians 6: 11–12)*

Divergent Christian teachings about war

Different Churches have different views about war. Because Quakers are against any form of war, they therefore do not believe in holy war:

> ❝We are a people that follow after those things that make for peace, love, and unity; it is our desire that others' feet may walk in the same, and do deny and bear our testimony against all strife, and wars. ❞
> *(Margaret Fell, 1660; known as the 'mother of Quakerism')*

As discussed in 4.5, some denominations (for example the Catholic Church and the Church of England) believe that war can sometimes be justified:

> ❝Resistance of evil may be and often is a positive duty [...] to yield to pressure in the face of certain aspects of evil [...] would imply a weak and sinful compliance [...] the true conclusion is not "peace at any price" but "righteousness at any cost". ❞
> *(Church of England)*

However, whilst they might feel that war can be justified in some circumstances, most Christians today do not believe in holy war. They would argue that God would not command a war, nor would God take sides in a war. This does not mean that war is never justified, just that religious reasons for war are never justified. In a statement condemning the Crusades which took place from 1095CE to 1291CE, during which time Christian armies massacred Muslim civilians among others in the name of a holy war, Pope John Paul II said:

> ❝... we cannot fail to recognise the infidelities to the Gospel committed by some of our brethren, especially during the second millennium. Let us ask pardon for the divisions which have occurred among Christians, for the violence some have used in the service of the truth and for the distrustful and hostile attitudes sometimes taken towards the followers of other religions. ❞
> *(Pope John Paul II)*

C Some denominations refer to themselves as an 'army', for example the 'Jesus Army', believing that doing good works and spreading the gospel is a battle against evil in the world

This quotation is saying that doing nothing when there is evil going on is just as bad as the evil itself. What do you think? **SUPPORT**

How do non-religious people view holy war?

Non-religious people, including atheists and Humanists, reject the notion of a holy war. There are different reasons for this:

- If there is no God, then there can be no holy war.
- God is used to justify what is really man's will, not God's.
- Using force to convert other people takes aware their religious freedom.
- Even if God does exist, why would a loving God support one side against another?

Christian responses

Christians do not share the non-religious view that there is no God, however in other respects, Christians today would agree with the non-religious criticisms of holy war: God's name can often be used to justify unlawful actions; spreading the gospel should be an invitation rather than being achieved by force; and God loves all people, not just a chosen few.

However, many Christians believe there is a 'spiritual' holy war going on (see page 124) in which they need to fight in the name of God against evil and injustice. Whilst non-religious people also want to bring an end to evil in the world, they do not believe this is a war with religious or spiritual significance.

BUILD YOUR SKILLS

1. Look back at 4.5. Can you explain the difference between a just war and a holy war?

2. What are the aims of a holy war? Make a list and explain each one in your own words.

3. a Create a diagram which summarises the different Christian and non-religious arguments about holy war. Its aim should be to help you remember each argument.
   b Next to each argument, make notes about how strong an argument it is and why.

4. The teachings about holy war in the Old Testament seem to be different to the teachings about holy war in the New Testament. Can you find out why most Christians do not believe this is a contradiction?

SUMMARY

- Holy wars are about defending and spreading a religious belief.
- Atheists, Humanists, and most Christians disapprove of the notion of holy wars.
- Many holy wars took place in the past.
- Most Christians believe that a true holy war is a spiritual battle against evil.

EXAM-STYLE QUESTIONS

b Explain **two** reasons why a holy war may or may not be important to a religious believer. (4)

d 'There is no such thing as a holy war.'
Evaluate this statement considering arguments for and against. In your argument you should:
  - refer to Christian teachings
  - refer to non-religious points of view
  - reach a justified conclusion. (12)

Weapons of mass destruction

What are weapons of mass destruction?

Weapons of mass destruction (WMD) are capable of killing and injuring thousands of people, and destroying cities and the natural landscape. It is almost impossible to use them without killing civilians, even if the target is a military one. WMD are often launched and controlled from a distance, as missiles, bombs, or drones. The person who releases the weapon may be on the other side of the world and would not experience the effect of the weapon. Usually, WMD attacks do not involve soldiers fighting at all.

There are four main types of WMD:

- **Nuclear weapons:** these can destroy all life and buildings in their range and often produce radioactive fall-out which kills people for years afterwards.
- **Biological weapons:** these use living bacteria and viruses, such as tuberculosis and anthrax, to infect and eventually kill people. Only those with protective clothing or shelters can survive.
- **Chemical weapons:** these use non-living poisons, such as mustard gas, to cause widespread death and injury.
- **Radiological weapons:** these are bombs that produce radioactive material to kill people and contaminate wide areas.

How do Christians respond to the problems and benefits of WMD?

Problems of WMD

Some Christians believe that WMD are unacceptable because:

- they are extremely difficult, if not impossible, to control
- they do not comply with the Just War theory because they cause disproportionate and indiscriminate destruction
- they go against Christian beliefs about the sanctity of life and **stewardship** – the need to protect and nurture the earth
- they kill and injure innocent civilians.

Benefits of WMD

Some Christians believe that, in certain circumstances, the possession of nuclear weapons is acceptable because:

- nuclear weapons can act as a deterrent – it would be foolish to attack a country that has them
- simply having nuclear weapons is enough to secure peace – they will never need to be used.

SPECIFICATION FOCUS

Christian attitudes to weapons of mass destruction (WMD): Christian teachings and responses to the problems and benefits of WMD; Christian attitudes towards the use of such weapons, including interpretations of Deuteronomy 20; non-religious attitudes (including atheist and Humanist) and the application of ethical theories, such as utilitarianism which supports the acquisition of weapons of mass destruction, and Christian responses to them.

A Hands blistered by mustard gas, used in the Second Italo-Ethiopian War (1935–36)

To say that WMD act as a **deterrent** means they frighten enemies away. **SUPPORT**

'There is no point in having nuclear weapons that will never be used'. What do you think? **STRETCH**

How do Christians respond to WMD?

The Catholic Church

The Catholic Church is opposed to the existence of WMD. WMD, they argue, can never be used in a just war because they involve the killing and maiming of innocent civilians. So, even if war is sometimes justified, the use of WMD is never justified:

> ❝In a nuclear war there would be no victors, only victims. The truth of peace requires that all [...] strive for a progressive and concerted nuclear **disarmament**.❞
> *(Pope Benedict XVI, World Day of Peace 2006)*

B 1972; The US used bombs containing napalm, a sticky, highly flammable chemical, in their bombing raids on Vietnam during the Vietnam War

The Church of England

The Church of England, whilst it regards the use of nuclear weapons as unjustifiable, believes that owning nuclear weapons is necessary. This is because if the UK did not possess nuclear weapons they would not be able to defend themselves against countries that do:

> ❝... the Synod rejected unilateral nuclear disarmament and accepted the duty of the British government to maintain adequate forces to deter nuclear aggression.❞
> *(Ethical Investment Advisory Group: Defence investments policy, May 2010)*

C A demonstration by religious groups against nuclear weapons, Parliament Square, London, July 2016

Deuteronomy 20

The Old Testament book of Deuteronomy was written 600 years or so before Jesus was born. Among other things, it records the events of 1000 years earlier. The book contains what seems to be God's instruction to the armies of Israel to carry out the mass destruction of the nations they encounter:

> ❝However, in the cities of the nations the Lord your God is giving you as an inheritance, **do not leave alive anything that breathes**. Completely destroy them [...] as the Lord your God has commanded you.❞
> *(Deuteronomy 20: 16–17)*

Many Christians believe that God did order the destruction of these nations, because the Bible describes the event, and they believe the Bible is the word of God. Other Christians would interpret this differently, and argue that this story depicts the victory of God's people, rather than the will of God to destroy others.

Many Christians on both sides, however, would still not use passages like these to endorse WMD today. The idea of complete destruction of one's enemies was the popular understanding of the meaning of war at the time the book of Deuteronomy was written. It is not a view that many Christians would accept any longer, even if (like the Church of England), they believe owning nuclear weapons is a necessary evil in an imperfect world. However, some Christians do.

USEFUL TERMS

Disarmament: reducing, withdrawing, or abolishing weapons

Stewardship: looking after something so it can be passed on to the next generation

Weapons of mass destruction: biological, chemical, and nuclear weapons that can cause widespread damage and kill thousands of people

How do non-religious people regard WMD?

Some non-religious people may argue in favour of possessing WMD as a deterrent. However, many are opposed to WMD. Famous atheist Bertrand Russell was one of the founders of the Campaign for Nuclear Disarmament (CND), which advocates for worldwide nuclear disarmament. There is no strict Humanist perspective on WMD. They will consider the evidence and the potential consequences when deciding where they stand.

Christian responses

Many Christians agree with Russell on the wrongness of WMD. For example, the CND, of which Russell was a member, also has a branch for Christians who want to witness to their faith through campaigning for nuclear disarmament.

How do ethical theories apply to WMD?

Utilitarianism

Utilitarianism is the theory that the right thing to do is whatever brings the greatest amount of happiness to the greatest number of people. A utilitarian viewpoint would support the acquisition of WMD because:

- having a deterrent keeps people safe and maintains the principle of 'the greatest happiness for the greatest number'
- the cost of WMD is small compared with the protection they bring.

However, a utilitarian may oppose WMD because:

- They may cause destruction that is not in the best interests of the majority of people
- WMD and war are costly in terms of finance and resource.

Situation ethics

Joseph Fletcher, who first suggested situation ethics, supported the bombing of Hiroshima and Nagasaki by the US in 1945, even though it caused the death of approximately 200,000 people, because it brought about the end of the Second World War. He argued that the greater good of ending the war was worth more than the lives lost in the bombing – so this was, in his view, the most loving action in the situation.

USEFUL TERM

Utilitarianism: the belief that the right course of action is the one that will produce the greatest happiness of the greatest number of people

D In 1945, the US dropped an atomic bomb on Hiroshima, Japan, devastating an area of five square miles around the city

SUMMARY

- Weapons of mass destruction cause widespread damage and can kill thousands of people.
- Some Christians believe WMD are needed as a deterrent to maintain peace.
- Others think WMD do not fit with the Just War theory and should be banned.

BUILD YOUR SKILLS

1   What are weapons of mass destruction?

SUPPORT

2   'The use of WMD is sometimes justified.' Make a list of arguments for and against this statement, including arguments from Christians, non-religious people, and ethical theories. Which is the strongest argument and why? Which is the weakest and why? Write a short conclusion, explaining your reasons.

EXAM-STYLE QUESTIONS

a   Outline **three** problems of WMD. (3)

b   Explain **two** reasons why many Christians do not support the use of WMD. (4)

4.8 Issues surrounding conflict

What are the issues surrounding conflict?

In 4.3, we looked at the main factors that cause conflict between nations, including fear, economics, and national pride. However, conflict can also occur on a smaller scale; in families, communities and between political groups within a nation. If a conflict remains unresolved, there are several key issues that can arise.

Violence

Violence is the intentional use of force or power against oneself, another person, or a group. Violence is most often thought of as a physical act, but it can also be emotional or psychological.

The underlying causes of violence are thought to include poverty, inequality, substance abuse, living in a violent culture, and/or severe mental health issues. However, it is not always clear why violence occurs. For example, in 2012 68-year-old Alan Greaves was on his way to church in Sheffield when two men made an unprovoked and brutal attack on him. He died three days later from severe head injuries (see page 131). Violence can devastate families and communities.

War

War is when two or more groups of people use violence against each other on a large scale. War is one way that some nations and groups choose to resolve conflict – for instance, the 'winner' gains access to the territory or resources that two nations were fighting over. Modern weapons can mean that violence carried out in a time of war is extreme. For example, over 70 million people died during World War II. Whole nations can be left in turmoil following this kind of conflict.

Terrorism

Terrorism is the unlawful use of violence, including against innocent civilians, to achieve a political or religious goal. Terrorism has been carried out by a wide range of political and religious groups for a variety of reasons over hundreds of years.

One example from British history is during 'the Troubles', a period of about 30 years of violence beginning in the late 1960s between Catholics and Protestants. An Irish military organization of Catholics called the Provisional Irish Republican Army carried out a series of violent attacks in an attempt to drive the British out of Ireland. Several Protestant terrorist organisations were formed in response, for example the Ulster Defence Association, who also used violence to fight against Irish republicanism in a bid to stay part of Britain.

A significant terrorist attack in the UK was the suicide bomb attacks in central London on 7 July 2005 in which 52 civilians were killed and over 700 were injured while using public transport at rush hour. The attacks were carried out by four Islamist extremists, who left messages suggesting they carried out the attacks because of Western violence against Muslims across the world. Specifically mentioned was the war in Iraq.

see page 131

SPECIFICATION FOCUS

Christian attitudes to issues surrounding conflict: Christian teachings and responses to the nature and history of problems involved in conflict – violence, war, and terrorism, including Luke 6: 27–31; how Christians have worked to overcome these issues; non-religious (including atheist and Humanist) views towards the issues surrounding conflict and Christian responses to them.

USEFUL TERMS

Terrorism: the unlawful use of violence, including against innocent civilians, to achieve a political or religious goal

Violence: the intentional use of force or power against oneself, another person, or a group

A In 1984, a Provisional IRA bomb exploded in the Grand Hotel, Brighton. Five people died and 34 were injured. Leading politicians staying there, including Margaret Thatcher, survived

129

Christian responses to the problems of violence, war and terrorism

Christians believe that Jesus is a peacemaker (see 4.2), and therefore violence, war, and terrorism is not part of God's plan for the world. Though suffering is a part of life, Christians believe that God will one day bring suffering to an end (see 1.8).

After the murder of French Catholic priest Father Jacques Hamel by alleged Islamic terrorists in 2016, Pope Francis said, 'Yes, it's war [...] when I speak of war [...] I am not speaking of a war of religions, religions don't want war. The others want war' (*Daily Mail, 27 July 2016*). The Pope's words express the idea that the existence of violence and terrorist acts isn't something that is endorsed by Christianity, Islam, or any other religion.

B Father Jacques Hamel was murdered during morning mass in France in 2016

Jesus' teaching on love for enemies

Jesus gives advice to those who experience conflict:

> **Love your enemies**, do good to those who hate you, bless those who curse you, pray for those who mistreat you. If someone slaps you on one cheek, turn to them the other also. If someone takes your coat, do not withhold your shirt from them. Give to everyone who asks you, and if anyone takes what belongs to you, do not demand it back. **Do to others what you would have them do to you.**
> *(Luke 6: 27–31)*

Do you agree or disagree with the teaching in *Luke 6: 27–31*? Say why, or why not.

Some people would oppose this teaching because:

- it could allow the strong to trample on the weak
- it may keep the poor oppressed
- it allows the aggressor to always 'win'.

However, many Christians would support it because:

- it stops people from responding aggressively
- it encourages people to display love and forgiveness
- a loving response could lead to peace and avoid conflict.

How have Christians worked to overcome issues surrounding conflict?

The Corrymeela Community

Many Christians are involved in work to bring about peace and overcome the issues caused by conflict. For example, the Corrymeela Community is a Christian community in Northern Ireland whose aim is to bring about healing and reconciliation between the Catholics and Protestants who were on opposite sides of 'the troubles' in the 1970s, 80s and 90s. They have a village where people from different communities come together to learn the skills of reconciliation and peace-building which they can then take back to their own communities.

Maureen Greaves

On Christmas Eve in 2012, 68-year-old social worker Alan Greaves was brutally attacked by two men on the way to Midnight Mass at St Saviour's Church in Sheffield, and later died in hospital. As Alan's wife, Maureen, sat at his bedside on Christmas Day she remembers that she started to pray: 'And I thought Alan would forgive them. It's Christmas Day. I didn't want to carry the anger, all that destructive anger, in my life'.

Exactly one year after Alan's murder, the congregation of St Saviour's met where Alan was killed for a short ceremony of remembrance. Maureen asked people to pray for Alan and his family, but also for his killers.

 How do Maureen Greaves' actions relate to Jesus' teaching in *Luke 6*? **SUPPORT**

 CASE STUDY: CORRIE TEN BOOM

Corrie ten Boom was a Dutch Christian who, along with her family, helped many Jews during the Second World War to escape the Nazi Holocaust. Because of this, she herself was imprisoned in Ravensbrück concentration camp.

After the war, she met the soldier who had been her guard at the camp. At first she could not shake his hand, but then remembered Jesus' teaching and prayed for God's help to forgive him. Shaking his hand, she said, 'I forgive you, brother, with all my heart.'

C Corrie ten Boom

Non-religious views on the issues around conflict

Humanists believe that people should use their intelligence and reason to overcome any instincts they may have to act aggressively to another person. They would also look sceptically at the reasons given by any government who seeks conflict, as a key issue in conflict can be how well all facts are considered and communicated. The vast majority of non-religious people would oppose violence and terrorism, though they may support the idea of war if it is the lesser evil in a given situation. As we have seen in 4.3, some non-religious people would blame religions for violence and extremism.

Christian responses to non-religious views on the issues around conflict

Christians would agree with many of these non-religious views. However, they might argue that ignorance and misinterpretation of religious teachings cause some individuals or groups to commit acts of violence or terrorism. Virtually all Christian denominations, for example, have denounced the Ku Klux Klan, who self-identify as Christian.

 BUILD YOUR SKILLS

1 With a partner, identify three problems caused by conflict and the impact these can have.

2 Choose either the Corrymeela Community or Corrie ten Boom to research further. What issues surrounding conflict do they try to overcome, and how?

SUMMARY

- Many Christians believe violence only brings about more violence.

- Terrorism is an act of violence, usually carried out against civilians, intended to cause harm and fear.

- Christian individuals work to overcome such issues through reconciliation and forgiveness.

 EXAM-STYLE QUESTIONS

a Outline **three** Christian beliefs about conflict. (3)

d 'Terrorism is impossible to overcome.'
Evaluate this statement considering arguments for and against. In your argument you should:
  - refer to Christian teachings
  - refer to non-religious points of view
  - reach a justified conclusion. (12)

Revision

BUILD YOUR SKILLS

Look at the list of 'I can' statements below and think carefully about how confident you are. Use the following code to rate each of the statements. Be honest!

Green – very confident. What is your evidence for this?

Orange – quite confident. What is your target? Be specific.

Red – not confident. What is your target? Be specific.

A self-assessment revision checklist is available on *Kerboodle*

I can...

- Explain reasons why most Christians would choose peace over war
- Describe situations in which some Christians would say war is necessary
- Describe what peacemaking is and what the Bible says about it
- List different ways in which Christian groups work for peace
- Describe what conflict is and give examples of conflicts
- Explain the factors that often lead to conflict
- Explain what Christians say about the causes of conflict
- Explain why non-religious people believe religion is a cause of conflict
- Describe what pacifism is and what Christianity says about it
- List Christian groups that take a pacifist stance
- Describe what passive resistance is
- Give examples of passive resistance in action

- Explain what is meant by just war
- Give examples of biblical teachings about just war
- Describe the conditions necessary for just war
- Explain problems with the Just War theory
- Explain what is meant by holy war
- Give examples of holy wars
- Explain what Christianity teaches about holy war
- Describe how non-religious people view holy war
- Explain what weapons of mass destruction are and give examples of their use
- Explain Christian beliefs about weapons of mass destruction
- Describe how non-religious people view weapons of mass destruction
- Explain what Christianity teaches about the issues surrounding conflict
- Explain what terrorism is and how Christians respond to it.

Exam practice

On these exam practice pages you will see example answers for each of the exam question types: **a**, **b**, **c**, and **d**. You can find out more about these on pages 6–10.

• Question 'a'

*Question **a** is AO1 – this tests your knowledge and understanding.*

> (a) Outline **three** Christian teachings about peace. (3)

Student response

Pray, forgive people, do not judge.

Improved student response

Pray for those who persecute you, forgive people as you have been forgiven, do not judge or you will be judged.

 Over to you! Give yourself three minutes on the clock and have a go at answering this question. Remember, this question type requires you to provide three facts or short ideas: you don't need to explain them or express any opinions.

✓ **WHAT WENT WELL**

This student has touched on three Christian teachings about peace.

❗ **HOW TO IMPROVE**

It's not clear enough how the elements in this answer are Christian teachings. An even better answer would give a little more detail. Have a look at the 'improved student response' for suggested corrections.

• Question 'b'

*Question **b** is AO1 – this tests your knowledge and understanding.*

> (a) Explain **two** ways that Christians work for peace. (4)

Student response

Christian organisations campaign against oppression and keep people informed of injustices around the world.

Improved student response

Christian organisations such as the World Council of Churches work for peace by bringing different groups together to try to solve disputes and heal divisions. They also campaign against racism and injustice. Pax Christi International tries to force governments to work more closely for peace through economic and social justice: 'vicious cycles of violence and injustice can be broken.'

 Over to you! Give yourself four minutes on the clock and have a go at answering this question. Remember, in order to 'explain' something, you need to **develop** your points. See page 9 for a reminder of how to do this.

✓ **WHAT WENT WELL**

This student has correctly named two ways that Christians work for peace.

❗ **HOW TO IMPROVE**

The answer would be improved if the student gave specific examples and was more precise about what Christians do and why. Developed points require an example or extra detail to be added. See the 'improved student response' opposite for suggested corrections.

• Question 'c'

Question c is AO1 – this tests your knowledge and understanding.

> (c) Explain **two** different Christian responses to the possession of weapons of mass destruction. In your answer you must refer to a source of wisdom and authority. (5)

Student response

Some Christians believe that WMD are unacceptable because they are difficult to control and can kill civilians. This is against biblical teaching on not killing innocent people. However, other Christians believe that possession of WMDs can benefit a nation.

Improved student response

Many Christians, including Catholics, believe that WMD are unacceptable because it goes against the teaching of the Bible that people should not murder (Exodus 20). They are difficult to control, which means that the lives of innocent civilians and the environment are threatened.

However, other Christians, for example members of the Church of England, believe that possession of WMDs can benefit a nation because they can deter a would-be aggressor and secure peace.

 Over to you! Give yourself five minutes on the clock and have a go at answering this question. Remember, you need to write two developed points, one of which needs to be supported by a source of wisdom and authority.

 WHAT WENT WELL

This student has correctly identified two different Christian beliefs and has referred to the Bible.

 HOW TO IMPROVE

This response could be improved with more detail – particularly in relation to the second point, which is currently not explained. The student could also make it clearer which teaching in the Bible they are referring to. See the 'improved student response' opposite for suggested corrections.

• Question 'd'

Question d is AO2 – this tests your ability to evaluate.

> (d) 'Christians should always support a holy war.' Evaluate this statement considering arguments for and against. In your response you should:
> • refer to Christian teachings
> • refer to non-religious points of view
> • reach a justified conclusion. (12)

Student response

Some Christians believe that the Bible supports going to war. Jesus said that he 'did not come to bring peace, but a sword' (Matthew 10: 34). They claim that it is right to fight in a war to protect people, as long as it is just. The Church of England seems to agree with this, claiming that 'resistance of evil may be and often is a positive duty'.

However, other Christians are against war because the Bible says 'Do not murder' (Exodus 20) and encourages Christians to love their enemies.

Perhaps the best conclusion is to say there are good arguments both ways and so participation in a war is an individual and personal choice.

Improved student response

A holy war is one in which religion is the driving force. Some Christians believe that the Bible supports holy war. Jesus called his followers to arms when he said 'I do not come to bring peace, but a sword' (Matthew 10: 34), which means that his teachings and example will bring division and conflict among people. Also, in Joshua 6 God seems to lead Joshua into battle. It could be argued, therefore, that if the Bible supports holy war, then so should Christians.

However, most Christians today do not support the idea of holy war, even though there are many who support war in general. These Christians would claim that Jesus in Matthew 10 is not advocating war, but is concentrating on the real holy war, which is the spiritual battle against the powers of evil, involving spiritual weapons, rather than physical weapons. The New Testament says: 'our struggle is not against flesh and blood, but against the powers of this dark world'.

Whilst they would also want to fight evil in the world, non-religious people are against holy war – both physical and spiritual – because they do not believe in God or that he would command an army of people. They also believe it is wrong to use force to spread religious faith.

In conclusion, Christians should be able to make an individual and personal decision about whether to fight a 'spiritual' holy war against evil in the world, but the evidence in support of a physical holy war is less convincing.

 Over to you! Give yourself twelve minutes on the clock and have a go at answering this question. Remember to refer back to the original statement in your writing when you give different points of view, and make sure you cover each of the bullet points given in the question.

 WHAT WENT WELL

The student has attempted to include two sides of the argument, with reference to Christian teachings.

 HOW TO IMPROVE

The student has answered the question as if it is asking about war in general, when in fact it is asking about holy war. Also, non-religious viewpoints have not been included. Have a look at this improved version of the student response.

BUILD YOUR SKILLS

In your exams, you'll need to make sure you use religious terminology correctly. Do you know the meaning of the following important terms for this topic?

peacemaker

conflict

Just War theory

justice

situation ethics

forgiveness

holy war

Humanist

weapons of mass destruction

pacifism

reconciliation

utilitarianism

passive resistance

atheist

terrorism

Glossary

39 Articles of Religion a historical record of beliefs (or 'doctrines') held by the Church of England

adultery a couple having sex even though one (or both) of them is married to someone else

advent a season of preparation for Christmas

aggressor person, group or country that is the first to attack another

agnostic someone who believes it is not possible to know whether or not God exists

Alpha a course run by churches and local Christian groups which enables people to find out more about the Christian faith in a relaxed setting

anoint apply oil to a person's head as a sign of holiness and God's approval

apartheid system in South Africa which segregated and discriminated against people according to their race

ascension going up into heaven

atheist someone who does not believe in the existence of God

atonement the action of restoring a relationship; in Christianity, Jesus' death and resurrection restores the relationship between God and human beings

atrocity extremely cruel or barbaric attack, usually involving violence

baptism the Christian ceremony that welcomes a person into the Christian community

begotten born of

benevolence all-good

blasphemy disrespect towards God or something considered sacred

charismatic a power given by God, e.g. inspired teaching

charity giving to those in need

civil disobedience refusing to comply with certain laws as a peaceful form of protest against them

conflict a serious disagreement

conscientious objector someone who refuses to serve in the armed forces for ethical reasons

conservation protecting something from being damaged or destroyed

convert to change from one set of beliefs to another

creationism the belief that the world was created in a literal six days and that Genesis is a scientific/historical account of the beginning of the world

creed a statement of firmly held beliefs; for example, the Apostles' Creed or the Nicene Creed

crucifixion being nailed to a cross and left to die

cybercrime crime committed online

Day of Judgement time when God assesses a person's life and actions

denominations the name given to the main groups within the Church

deterrence discouragement from doing something, for example carrying out a criminal act

disarmament reducing, withdrawing, or abolishing weapons

ecumenism a movement that tries to bring different Christian denominations closer together

environment the surroundings in which plants and animals live and on which they depend for life

epiphany a moment of suddenly revealing something surprising or great; in the Christian calendar, Epiphany is a celebration of the revelation of Jesus

Eschatology an area of Christian theology which is concerned with life after death

Eucharist the ceremony commemorating the Last Supper, involving bread and wine; also called Holy Communion or Mass

evangelism preaching the gospel in order to attract new believers

execution carrying out a sentence of death by killing a person

fair trial a public hearing by an independent tribunal established by law, which takes place within a reasonable time

forgiveness pardoning a person for a wrong committed against you; in a Christian context, forgiveness doesn't always come about because the person deserves to be forgiven, but out of love, mercy, and grace

free will having the freedom to choose what to do

grace undeserved love

heaven place of eternal paradise where Christians believe they will spend the afterlife

hell place of punishment and separation from God

Holy Spirit the Spirit of God, which gives the power to understand and worship

Holy war war to spread a religious belief or to defend that belief

Holy week the week before Easter

human rights rights which all human beings are entitled to

Humanist a non-religious person who looks to reason and empathy in order to live a meaningful life

humanity all human beings

immortal soul a soul that lives on after the death of the physical body

incarnation to take on flesh; God becomes a human being

intercession prayers for those who are suffering

Jesus Christ the Son of God, who came into the world as a human being

Just War theory a set of conditions that need to be met in order for a war to be justified

justice doing what is right and fair based on the law

law guidelines as to how people should behave; the rules that govern society

liturgical a set form of worship, usually following agreed words

local church a meeting place for local believers and the community of believers who gather there

looting stealing goods from shops and houses, usually during a war or a riot

mediator person who tries to help those in conflict reach agreement

mission sending individuals or groups to spread the Christian message

missionary a person who preaches and invites people to convert to the Christian faith

moral evil suffering caused by humans, such as war

nativity the birth of someone

natural evil suffering caused by natural events, such as earthquakes

non-liturgical a form of worship which is not set

Offender Behaviour Programme (OBP) scheme intended to reduce reoffending by tackling issues associated with crime

omnipotence all-powerful

outreach an activity to provide services to people in need

pacifism the belief that war can never be justified and that conflicts should be settled peacefully

pacifist someone who believes that war and violence are never justified

parish a community of local believers within a particular denomination

passive resistance non-violent opposition to something; this may involve going against certain laws

peacemaker someone who works for peace and an end to conflict

Pentecostalism a Protestant movement that puts special emphasis on a direct and personal relationship with God through the Holy Spirit

persecution the ill-treatment of an individual or group, usually on the grounds of religion, politics or ethnicity

pilgrimage a journey to a religious or holy place

prayer a way of communicating with God

prophecy a message from God in which he communicates his will

protection keeping someone or something safe from harm, for example criminal activity

punish impose a penalty on someone for doing something wrong

purgatory a place where the souls of the dead are cleansed and prepared for heaven

reconcile restore friendly, peaceful or agreeable relations with someone

reconciliation restoring peace and friendship between individuals or groups

reformation changing something (or someone) for the better

rehabilitate restore someone back to a law-abiding life

reoffend return to criminal behaviour

repentance to say sorry for, and turn away from, any wrongdoing

restorative justice a form of rehabilitation in which criminals are given the opportunity to meet victims of crime

resurrection rising from the dead; also the view that after death God recreates a new body in a heavenly place

retaliation returning an attack; similar to revenge

retribution punishment given in revenge for a wrong that has been done

sacrament an important Christian ceremony

salvation being saved from sin and the consequences of sin; going to heaven

Satan 'the adversary'; one of God's angels who rebelled against the rule of God

sermon a talk or teaching from a church leader

shrine a holy place

sin anything that prevents a relationship with God, either because the person does something they shouldn't, or neglects to do something they should

situation ethics ethical decisions are made according to the specific context of the decision

spiritual gifts gifts given by God to believers, e.g. speaking in 'tongues', a special language

stewardship looking after something so it can be passed on to the next generation

terrorism the unlawful use of violence, including against innocent civilians, to achieve a political or religious goal

terrorist person who uses unlawful violence or threats to harm or injure people

torture inflicting severe pain on someone

treason being disloyal to one's country by plotting to overthrow the government or ruler

trial by jury a trial where the jury's decision directs the actions of the judge

Trinity God as one being, in three persons

universalism the belief that because of the love and mercy of God everyone will go to heaven

utilitarianism the belief that the right course of action is the one that will produce the greatest happiness of the greatest number of people

vale of soul-making an environment in which human beings can overcome evil by making good choices

vigil staying awake at night in order to pray; also the name given to the celebration of a festival on the eve before the festival itself

violence the intentional use of force or power against oneself, another person or a group

vision seeing or hearing someone or something holy

weapons of mass destruction biological, chemical, and nuclear weapons that can cause widespread damage and kill thousands of people

worship believers expressing love and respect for, and devotion to, God

Index

Acknowledgements

We are grateful to the authors and publishers for use of extracts from their titles and in particular for the following:

Scripture quotations taken from the **Holy Bible, New International Version Anglicised** Copyright © 1979, 1984, 2011 Biblica. Used by permission of Hodder & Stoughton Ltd, an Hachette UK company. All rights reserved. 'NIV' is a registered trademark of Biblica UK trademark number 1448790.

Excerpts from **Catechism of the Catholic Church**, http://www.vatican.va/archive/ccc_css/archive/catechism/ccc_toc.htm (Strathfield, NSW: St Pauls, 2000). © Libreria Editrice Vaticana. Reproduced with permission from The Vatican.

St Augustine: in *Nicene and Post-Nicene Fathers*, First Series, Vol. 2. Translated by Marcus Dods. Revised and edited by Kevin Knight, http://www.newadvent.org/fathers/120101.htm (New Advent, 2009). © 2009 Kevin Knight. Reproduced with permission from Kevin C. Knight.

The Church of England: *Countering Terrorism*, report September 2005 (Archbishops' Council, 2005). © Archbishops' Council. Reproduced with permission from The Archbishops' Council.

The Church of England: *Ethical Investment Advisory Group: Defence investments policy*, May 2010, https://www.churchofengland.org/media/1376267/defence%20policy%20may%202010.pdf (Archbishops' Council, 2010). © Archbishops' Council. Reproduced with permission from The Archbishops' Council.

The Church of England: *Justice Issues & Prisons*, https://www.churchofengland.org/our-views/home-and-community-affairs/home-affairs-policy/justice-issues-prisons.aspx (Archbishops' Council, 2016). © Archbishops' Council. Reproduced with permission from The Archbishops' Council.

Michael Fitzgerald: The Times 9th October 2004, (The Times, 2004). Reproduced with permission from News Syndication.

Peter Lee: *To Fight or Not to Fight: the Christian's dilemma*, (AFCU, 2015). Reproduced with permission from P. Lee, King's College London.

The Methodist Church in Britain: *Methodist Conference Statement on Peace and War*, (The Methodist Church in Britain, 1957). © Trustees for Methodist Church Purposes. Reproduced with permission from The Methodist Church in Britain.

Pope Benedict XVI: *World Day of Peace*, speech 2006, https://w2.vatican.va/content/benedict- (The Vatican, 2006). © Libreria Editrice Vaticana. Reproduced with permission from The Vatican.

Pope Francis: speech 27th July 2016, (The Vatican, 2016). © Libreria Editrice Vaticana. Reproduced with permission from The Vatican.

Pope John Paul II: *Day of Pardon*, speech March 2000, (The Vatican, 2000). © Libreria Editrice Vaticana. Reproduced with permission from The Vatican.

Pope John XXIII: *Encyclical of Pope John XXIII on Establishing Universal Peace in Truth, Justice, Charity, and Liberty*, 11th April 1963, (The Vatican, 1963). © Libreria Editrice Vaticana. Reproduced with permission from The Vatican.

Quakers in Britain: *Quaker declaration to Charles II and parliament, 1660*, http://qfp.quaker.org.uk/passage/19-46/ (Quakers in Britain, 2016). Reproduced with permission from Quakers in Britain.

D. L. Smail and K. Gibson (eds): *Pope Urban II, Vengeance in Medieval Europe: a reader*, (University of Toronto Press, 2009). Reproduced with permission from University of Toronto Press.

C. Ten Boom: *The Hiding Place*, (Baker Publishing Group, 2010). Reproduced with permission from Baker Publishing Group.

We have made every effort to trace and contact all copyright holders before publication, but if notified of any errors or omissions, the publisher will be happy to rectify these at the earliest opportunity.

The publisher would like to thank the following for permission to use their photographs:

COVER: Eugene Sergeev/Alamy

contents/revision page backgrounds: mironov/Shutterstock; **p4:** Lolostock / Shutterstock; **p6:** Photoonlife / Shutterstock; **p7:** totallypic / Shutterstock; **p8:** Nikolaeva / Shutterstock; **p9:** SH-Vector / Shutterstock; **p10:** Tang Yan Song / Shutterstock; **p11:** Sutichak / Shutterstock; **p12:** mangostock / Shutterstock; **p13:** Art Directors & TRIP / Alamy Stock Photo; **p14:** Photobank gallery/Shutterstock; **p14:** Eugene Sergeev/Shutterstock; **p17:** The Baptism of Christ, c.1580-88 (oil on canvas), Veronese, (Paolo Caliari) (1528-88) / © Samuel Courtauld Trust, The Courtauld Gallery, London, UK / Bridgeman Images; **p18:** © Jeff Gilbert / Alamy Stock Photo; **p19:** Lisa S./Shutterstock; **p21:** robert_s/Shutterstock; **p22:** © Gregg Vignal / Alamy Stock Photo; **p23:** Amy Watts; p24: © AF archive / Alamy Stock Photo; **p25:** © Paul Rapson / Alamy Stock Photo; **p26:** © Archivart / Alamy Stock Photo; **p27:** Photobank gallery/Shutterstock; **p28:** © AF archive / Alamy Stock Photo; **p28:** Lokibaho/iStock; **p29:** Colin Underhill / Alamy Stock Photo; p30: Heritage Image Partnership Ltd / Alamy Stock Photo; **p31:** © Archivart / Alamy Stock Photo; **p32:** Samuel Cohen / Shutterstock; **p33:** Iakov Kalinin/Shutterstock; **p34:** Iulian Dragomir/Shutterstock; **p34:** Steve Skjold/Alamy Stock Photo; **p36:** WitthayaP/Shutterstock; **p36:** ZUMA Press, Inc. / Alamy Stock Photo; **p38:** Jorge Fajl/National Geographic Creative/Corbis; **p39:** Eugene Sergeev/Shutterstock; **p40:** © Design Pics Inc / Alamy Stock Photo; **p41:** Michaelpuche/Shutterstock; **p46:** majaiva / iStock; **p46:** Roger Bamber / Alamy Stock Photo; **p48:** majaiva / iStock; **p48:** Trinity Mirror / Mirrorpix / Alamy Stock Photo; **p50:** PRISMA ARCHIVO / Alamy Stock Photo; **p50:** classicpaintings / Alamy Stock Photo; p53: Justin Kase z04z / Alamy Stock Photo; **p53:** Maurice Crooks / Alamy Stock Photo; **p53:** hamburg_berlin / Shutterstock; **p54:** Heritage Image Partnership Ltd / Alamy Stock Photo; **p55:** Justin Nugent / Alamy Stock Photo; p55: STEVE LINDRIDGE / Alamy Stock Photo; **p56:** Panther Media GmbH / Alamy Stock Photo; **p57:** Alan Brine; **p58:** ASP Religion / Alamy Stock Photo; **p60:** Brian A Jackson / Shutterstock; **p60:** Roger Bamber / Alamy Stock Photo; **p61:** Michaelpuche / Shutterstock; **p62:** Justin Nugent / Alamy Stock Photo; **p63:** Photofusion/Universal Images Group via Getty Images; p64: Mark Harvey / Alamy Stock Photo; **p65:** Janine Wiedel Photolibrary / Alamy Stock Photo; **p66:** ralph hodgson / Alamy Stock Photo; **p67:** STEPHEN JAFFE/AFP/Getty Images; **p67:** photo.ua / Shutterstock; **p68:** RTimages / Shutterstock; **p69:** SCPhotos / Alamy Stock Photo; **p70:** AlexLMX / Shutterstock; **p70:** ZUMA Press, Inc. / Alamy Stock Photo; **p71:** Robert J Daveant / Shutterstock; **p71:** REUTERS / Alamy Stock Photo; **p76:** Skim New Media Limited / Alamy Stock Photo; **p76:** Nancy Bauer / Shutterstock; **p78:** Pontino / Alamy Stock Photo; **p79:** Art Directors & TRIP / Alamy Stock Photo; **p81:** Thoom / Shutterstock; **p82:** TerryHealy / Getty Images; p83: Mkucova / iStock; **p84:** Godong / Alamy Stock Photo; **p85:** Chokniti Khongchum / Shutterstock; **p86:** elenaleonova / Getty Images; **p86:**

Granger, NYC. / Alamy Stock Photo; **p87**: Mary Evans Picture Library / Alamy Stock Photo; **p88**: Muammar Awad/Anadolu Agency/Getty Images; **p89**: robertharding / Alamy Stock Photo; **p90**: Barry Lewis / Alamy Stock Photo; **p91**: KAREN MINASYAN/AFP/Getty Images; **p92**: The Resurrection of Christ and the Pious Women at the Sepulchre, 1442 (fresco), Angelico, Fra (Guido di Pietro) (c.1387–1455) / Museo di San Marco dell'Angelico, Florence, Italy / Bridgeman Images; **p93**: Amy Mikler / Alamy Stock Photo; **p94**: Borderlands / Alamy Stock Photo; **p95**: Alpha; **p97**: Peter Noyce GEN / Alamy Stock Photo; **p97**: Jim West / Alamy Stock Photo; **p98**: Vatican Pool/Getty Images; **p99**: epa european pressphoto agency b.v. / Alamy Stock Photo; **p101**: Rana Sajid Hussain/Pacific Press/LightRocket via Getty Images; **p101**: Frances Roberts / Alamy Stock Photo; **p102**: Sam Spickett / Christian Aid; **p108**: Ken Tannenbaum / Shutterstock; **p108**: Photos 12 / Alamy Stock Photo; **p110**: Photos 12 / Alamy Stock Photo; **p111**: DEA / G. DAGLI ORTI / Getty Images; **p112**: Zvonimir Atletic / Shutterstock; **p113**: World Council of Churches; **p113**: Pax Christi International; **p113**: amer ghazzal / Alamy Stock Photo; **p114**: Joseph Sohm / Shutterstock; **p114**: Trinity Mirror / Mirrorpix / Alamy Stock Photo; **p116**: INTERFOTO / Sammlung Rauch / Mary Evans; **p117**: Ken Tannenbaum / Shutterstock; **p118**: Bjanka Kadic / Alamy Stock Photo; **p119**: Pictorial Press Ltd / Alamy Stock Photo; **p120**: The Print Collector / Alamy Stock Photo; **p121**: epa european pressphoto agency b.v. / Alamy Stock Photo; **p121**: Universal Images Group North America LLC / DeAgostini / Alamy Stock Photo; **p123**: Mary Evans Picture Library ; **p124**: See Li / Alamy Stock Photo; **p126**: Everett Historical / Shutterstock; **p127**: REX/Shutterstock; **p127**: Peter Marshall / Alamy Stock Photo; **p128**: Ewing Galloway\UIG/REX/Shutterstock; **p129**: Trinity Mirror / Mirrorpix / Alamy Stock Photo; **p130**: epa european pressphoto agency b.v. / Alamy Stock Photo; **p131**: Frank Edwards/Fotos International/Getty Images